FIRST HAND:

AN EROTIC GUIDE
TO FISTING

FIRST HAND:
AN EROTIC GUIDE
TO FISTING

Tim Brough

**with an Introduction by
Jack Fritscher, PhD**

First Edition

A Boner Book
The Nazca Plains Corporation
Las Vegas, Nevada
2005

ISBN:1-887895-55-8

Published by,

The Nazca Plains Corporation ®
4640 Paradise Rd, Suite 141
Las Vegas NV 89109-8000

"Mapping the Genome of Leather S&M" was first published by Harold Cox
in an earlier millennium version in *Checkmate Incorporating
Dungeonmaster*, issue 33, November 2000; reprinted with permission of the
author, Jack Fritscher.
© 2005 Jack Fritscher

Original Artwork on pages 2 and 119
© 2005 Ed Moore, Washington DC
and is used by permission

Diagram of the Intestines on page 8 obtained from the
free clipart site; *www.classroomclipart.com*

Cover photography by Corwin

LEGAL NOTICE:

Hey, I am a writer, dammit. I'm not a medical doctor and I am not a lawyer. I have no legal or medical education. I got a degree in Communications and Theater Arts, for crying out loud. So, under no circumstances is anything in this book, regardless of its obvious or credited source, to be construed as medical counsel or the advice of a certified, licensed or recognized medical professional. Under no circumstances is anything in this book, regardless of its obvious or credited source to be construed a legal counsel or the advice of a certified, licensed or recognized legal professional.

The Publisher of this book is ALSO not a medical doctor and has no medical education. Under no circumstances is anything in this book, regardless of its obvious or credited source to be construed as medical counsel or the advice of a certified licensed or recognized medical professional. The Publisher of this book is not a lawyer and has no legal education. Under no circumstances is anything in this book, regardless of its obvious or credited source to be construed as legal counsel or the advice of a certified, licensed or recognized legal professional. The above also applies to all of the contributers to *First Hand*.

None of us takes responsibility for the actions a reader or their partner/participant/play-buddy may undertake after reading this book.

We trust that all parties will take the time to understand that any kind of kinky play carries with it dual elements of risk and responsibility, and undertakes their activities with those thoughts foremost in their minds.

Tim Brough
CYA, 2005

For Papa Joel,

For all your help proofreading, transcribing the tapes,
and for being my Aba dov.

Table Of Contents

A note from the author

Fisting, fist-fucking, and handballing are all terms applied to the sexual act of having someone's hand inserted into another's ass. After that, the definitions fly in all sorts of directions. Depending on whom you ask, fisting ranges from a divine sexual communion to the ultimate in physical domination and submission. Like all sexual activities, for a majority of the participants, the definition lies somewhere in the middle ground.

To an outsider, fisting can look like a terrifying and dangerous activity. Or it can plain just gross them out. The trick is in understanding that, when done with care and consensuality, fisting can bring incredible pleasures to both parties. When conducting the interviews for this book, I posed two main questions to each subject. The first was "What exactly is it that you get out of fisting?" The second was if they could describe their most memorable fisting experience. Descriptions of fisting frequently mentioned the *fullness* of being fisted as bottoms, or for the tops, the deep connections and warmth from having one's arm within the confines of another man's body.

The pleasure is not all physical. After all, if you really just wanted to engage in ass stuffing, there are plenty of dildos, butt plugs and vibrators on the market for that precise purpose. The mental satisfaction from allowing another man to share the physical intimacy of handballing can create psychological intimacy, as well. Fisting is both an act of strength and power, but above that, it is an act of gentility and caring. As it is with almost all forms of sex and sensuality, the partners need to share the kind of intimacy required to explore their sexual desires, and the trust to allow them to share in actions that, while pleasurable, need to be performed with caring and caution.

"Fisting is edge play to me, in that it's one of the most intimate opportunities to connect with another human being. Your fist, the arm, inside an individual, being able to feel the heartbeat, is quite intimate and very edgy play and it just excites the hell out of me. Edge play is play that has an element of danger to it and fisting can be dangerous, if it's not being done correctly." Master Z

There is something indescribably fulfilling about handballing. No matter which perspective you take in the commission of the activity, you as two become one more than in any other manner of play, and that includes fucking. I've heard men describing it as touching a man's heart from within. I've heard it compared to being lifted from the inside up. No matter how many adjectives are applied to the art, fisting matches flesh and spirit, binding the participants for the moment that their bodies are grafted together.

Grafting is also a term applied to horticulture, defined as to unite a shoot or bud with a growing plant by insertion, and usually with trees. Imagine, then, the limb of one man implanted into the flesh of another. Think of how that branch becomes forever a part of the tree it has grafted to, and use that metaphor as the manner that fisting binds the participants, be it the duration of the scene or for the superimposed commingling of their lives. Each part of the tree becomes stronger, firmer, by the creation of the graft.

It would help explain how fisting clubs become so successful, and why their members become so tightly knit. The Red Hankies of San Diego, the Philly Phists and Mid American Fists In Action (M.A.F.I.A.) have had such long and illustrious lives as gay male organizations (M.A.F.I.A. has been around since 1978). These ties bind strong and it is only a partial glimpse as to why active fisting fanatics are so devoted to their particular kink.

Still, everyone has to start somewhere. That's why I've taken on the task of writing and compiling this handbook (no pun intended). There will be those who will notice an absence of a chapter that deals with the hazards of drug and other substance abuse. Frankly, I ain't your Grand Dad. You go to a play party or a run and the poppers will be out, as well as a crowd at the beer tent. But we all know that drugs and alcohol mess up your sharpness and clarity, poppers can cause lung and brain damage, beer makes you stoopid and tweakers suck. With *Newsweek*, *National Public Radio* and *Rolling Stone* all running major stories about Crystal Meth addiction and the dangers of tweaking during 2005, you don't need me channeling Nancy Reagan or *South Park's* Mr. Garrisson. "Drugs are bad, m'kay?" As with all varieties of kink, Safe, Sane and Consensual still rules the sling, as does a hefty dose of common sense with a side helping of brains. Playing dirty doesn't mean playing dumb. End of rant....

The majority of the interviews for *First Hand* took place at various events across the country during spring and summer, 2005. These events included CLAW in Cleveland, International Mister Leather in Chicago, South Plains Leather in Dallas, and LA Leather Weekend, Los Angeles. Other interviews were conducted over the phone and a few via the Internet. Thanks to everybody who gave their time and voice to this project. My extra special thanks to Ed Klein of the Philly Phists, for allowing me to sit in on some of their club activities.

My thanks as always to friends there during the creation of this book, Daddy Ow, Russ, Masters Dennis, Gaines, Gerry, Jack Rinella, Thomas, both Alex K and Ironrod, Uncle Ed, Whiteknight.

I hope it allows a little light to enter where the sun don't usually shine. Or shines out of, depending on your thoughts about the subject.

MAPPING THE GENOME OF LEATHER S&M:
How Fisting and S&M Fringe Sex Entered the Homomasculine Mainstream

by Jack Fritscher, PhD
www.JackFritscher.com

Life is a learning to surrender control. We are born believing the double Human Fallacy: we have control; we have free will. Only to a point this side of Maya. We are amazing hand puppets of the gods, the force, the cosmos. We learn, through the hard-knock lessons life visits upon us, or the lessons we seek. If we remain *open*, we realize, while maybe bored in a bar, that to mature is to learn detachment from things as well as from ideas drummed into our heads when we were little boys.

The trend among 21st-century men is to simplify. Unload possessions and middle-class values. Travel without baggage across the digital divide of our butt. Fly across the geography of the planet. Climb up the geography of our bodies. Rearrange our recombinant DNA! Map the Genome of S&M!

Sex pleasure teaches psychic wisdom. When Fisting Tops and Fistable Bottoms open assholes, then hearts and minds also open. Incoming new concepts destroy old cautions and old taboos. We learn *The Way Out Is The Way In!* This is the code of the West only gay men know. This is the secret language of Hand Puppets. It's S&M Leather and Fetish. It's why the tasty word *orgasm* ends with *S-M*.

ENDGAME: FIST OF THE GENOME

Ain't there a hardon kick in purposely turning the opposite direction into a 1-way street and racing the Thrill Ride successfully to the next corner? You prove that the 1-way street can actually be a 2-way drive through a Sunday in the park with George, or Bob, or Bear. Maybe you're a 20'th century fox still wanting to drive on into the geography of the 21'st century going your own way.

Gays are a developing nation: a 4th-world subculture of eros. C21 gay men are sons of the Stonewall gay men. They liberated the 1960's into the 1970's Golden Age of Sexual Freedom that existed post-penicillin and pre-HIV. Vietnam ate men (including gay men) until the war ended in 1975. Threat of early death in war drove draft-age men into Fringe Heights of public sex. The more extravagantly gay a man was the less likely the Selective Service was to draft him for a killer or a victim in a useless war. You stand on the rich experience of those pioneer heroes.

You build your *man*stream future of rights, erotic vision, trust, and wisdom on the fraternal shoulders of previous generations. You affirm our wider-deeper-harder male history with the same insistence as women affirming female history. You keep on inventing the Brave New World of Homomasculinity.

Men's hands traditionally are for shaking, making, hunting, and open-handed slapping of dick. Inside the long and coded history of gay culture, gay hands are everything straight hands are - and then some! All men use their hands for jerking off. Ancient men in caves knew the secret bond when one man slipped his hand - finger by knuckle by fist - into another man. Men's hands know the sense of comradeship, of prisoner punishment-rape, of orgy, of ecstasy. Traditional initiation into the French Foreign Legion is a disciplined power-insert of fist-up-butt. "March or die!" starts with "Take it or leave!" I know, because in one of those nights at the Slot Hotel, South of Market in 1973, a former French Legionnaire told me so. (Gay wisdom teaches one to believe all stories told, because every man knows the stories he himself could tell, while true, would cause the naive to disbelieve.)

For readers not familiar with edge-pushing French Legionnaire S&M, or with Legionnaire extreme training, punishment, and torture - especially with Legionnaires' obsession with fists, fisticuffs, and gut-punching, I cannot recommend too highly *Legionnaire: My Five Years in the French Foreign Legion*, by Simon Murray, Times books, 1978. Murray writes frankly about beatings, torture, and punishment shit scenes; but when his code of honor suddenly draws the curtain over some brutal Legion scenes, gaydar immediately scans between his lines to fill in the nitty gritty that dare not speak its name. (Every gay man is skilled at this kind of literary interpretation; before Stonewall, gaydar was the way we all read historical novels and men's magazines for their hidden homo scenes, plots, and characters.) Murray receives credit for citing the great Gillo Pontecorvo's 1965 film *The Battle of Algiers* which graphically depicts Legionnaires' very creative approach to torture. Even though gay men get hard when torturing other men - and to the chagrin of queer academics, my research indicates that Legionnaires do not consider "men torturing men sexually" to be, well, homosexuality. For the homo twist on the Legion, check out gay saint Jean Genet who actually joined the French Foreign Legion, and Michel Foucault, habitue of Folsom Street and author of *Discipline and Punish* (1976), who only wished he could.

Beau Travail, directed by Claire Denis (2000), is probably the most sensual movie ever of the French Foreign Legion's discipline, prisons, and soldiers' bonding over biceps, helicopters, slow-motion male bodies exercising gymnastics and tai chi, "shaven-headed young giants"stripped nearly naked in the sun, helicopter rescues, and a sexually jealous sergeant stripped of his stripes in the military outpost. *Beau Travail*, actually, is Melville's *Billy Budd* moved from a Navy ship to the desert post in the Gulf of Djibouti, as the narrating officer reminisces about how splendid life used to be, before it went all wrong. Sound familiar? (Like the "Titanic 1970s.")

ONSCREEN FISTS IN THE CHUNNEL OF LOVE

On satellite dish, see *A Clockwork Orange*'s Malcolm MacDowell as the edgy Roman emperor in *I, Claudius*, a Bob Guccionne feature film produced for *Penthouse*. The plot revolves on Claudius' lurid, deep, and cruel fisting of a juicy young bridegroom. In 1981, *I, Claudius*, projected into straight pop culture a fisting consciousness that had long been lifestyle among gay men.

In 1972, *Born to Raise Hell*, the first gay S&M movie featuring fisting, piss, leather, and fringe play was premiered in a San Francisco movie theater at the corner of Powell and Market by producer Terry LeGrand and director Roger Earl. *Born to Raise Hell,* with its appealing stars and its best-selling photo book, became an instant classic in the 1970s, the wonderful decade devoted to discovery of Actual Gay Personality. Its fisting scene, which seems to start out consensually, made it as famous as its star, *Mr. Drummer*, Val Martin.

Pornstar Fred Halsted thought *Born*'s fisting scene got too real and went beyond consensual. Fred, who also wrote for my *Drummer*, was a hunky LA stud expert in directing leather sex, fisting (butts and faces), and esthetics. Maybe he was jealous that Earl and LeGrand's stars were so convincing. Earl-LeGrand are quite talented and they put "real" onscreen. In June 1989, in Europe, Mark Hemry and I, as Palm Drive Video, shot Earl-LeGrand's first two-camera shoot. Together, we created six very intense and - we can swear - very, very real, yet consensual, S&M videos: *The Argos Session (Amsterdam), Fit to Be Tied (Düsseldorf), Marks of Pleasure (Hamburg), Knast (Berlin), The Berlin Connection, Loose Ends of the Rope (Off the Autobahn)*. Halsted's porno-art films, *Sextool* and *L.A. Plays Itself* are in the permanent collection of the Museum of Modern Art. In 1978, filmmaker Wakefield Poole, fresh from *Boys in the Sand*, made the first totally dedicated fisting film, *Moving*, starring San Franciscans Terry Weekly and Top fistpig Peter Fisk (not Peter Fiske, Whipmeister).

FIST-O-PHOBIA: U.S. SENATE vs MAPPLETHORPE

Fist-o-phobia from fundamentalist straights took legendary S&M photographer, Robert Mapplethorpe, directly to the Supreme Court of free speech. Mapplethorpe's classic black-and-white shots of 1) a whip up his own leather-chapped butthole, and 2) beautiful round buns penetrated by a fist-to-the-wrist drove Republican senators so righteously angry in 1989 that Mapplethorpe's fist and other photographs became the media gay-scandal of the decade. Driven by a fist, the outraged Senate Republicans in the 1990s dared to defund the National Endowment for the Arts (NEA) and with it all gay-related works and fringe performances.

If rejection of fisting in art creates "censorship," then acceptance of fisting in life must lead to a whole lot of "freedom." Republican fundamentalists seem convinced that once a male learns the secret of his butt he'll never again be obedient to authority. Actually, forbidden gay sex always had a special edge-play thrill back when we were all John Rechy's *Sexual Outlaw,* because gay sex, down by law, was itself illegal.

FANTASY TRIP @ THE HOTEL ALABAMA

Isn't it more fun now that Alabama has outlawed dildos to think about taking your vacation in Alabama just so you can do a performance, ironically and really, using dozens of dildos at one time in your hotel room, knowing that any minute the Alabama troopers can barge in like Serbs into Kosovo? Or the US into Baghdad? The famous Robert Mapplethorpe, who was incidentally my bi-coastal lover, was a great Fisting Top who after finally himself going bottom, wrote me from New York on May 21, 1978, "It's midnight...I almost forgot to tell you. I let some creep stick his hand up my ass. I've been fisted— even came—but I think I prefer being the giver." Earlier, on April 10, 1978, on "Hotel Boulderado" letterhead, bored while shooting Allen Ginsberg in Colorado, *caro Roberto* finished his long letter to me with these words: "I'm going to turn off the lights and...muster up enough energy to 'Jack' off. I'm going to think about having my fist up your asshole while you...[deleted]...Love, Robert." When a genius wants to fist you, let him. Mapplethorpe Doppelganger twin, rocker Jim Morrison sang, "Ride the King Snake."

NY FISTS: THE MINESHAFT

Robert Mapplethorpe was a keystone figure at Wally Wallace's Mineshaft in New York's West Village. In 1989, Wally gave me a definitive 3-hour video interview about the history of the Mineshaft from the beginning in 1976 to its end in 1985. Plus he handed over copies of nearly 100 rare photographs taken in the "no-cameras" Mineshaft where, on the dramatically arranged 2-stories of platforms, slings, and porcelain tubs, men performed all the Greatest Hits on the Gay Adventure Sex List: feces to piss to fisting. Rex's famous black-and white drawing for the fist-o-rama of the Mineshaft featured a piss-thirsty leatherman with arms greased and ready.

The Mineshaft was, no doubt, the best public Fringe Pit devoted to fisting, S&M, scat-and-water sports in the whole history—no exaggeration—of the world: ancient to high tech to well into whatever comes in Century 21! The best Hollywood film featuring the Mineshaft culture was 1979's *Cruising*, directed by William (*The Boys in the Band, The Exorcist*) Friedkin and starring Al Pacino as a straight cop who gets caught up in the "Mineshaft Mystique." Friedkin actually cast the *Cruising* extras from the hottest Mineshaft regulars. A single-frame advance through the video of this once-highly-controversial film reveals an underlying *gay documentary* of many Night-Time Sex Stars and even some well-known pornstars lending themselves to the true feeling of those sweet Mineshaft nights. Wally Wallace cannot receive enough praise for his actual genius in creating the expressionist stage of the world-famous Mineshaft. He was the premier "performance producer" of Fringe Sex in the Golden Age when everyone was an erotic Performance Artist.

FISTING BALLET: CANARIES IN THE MINESHAFT

When the canaries in the Mineshaft died, it was time to cut and run. Shortly, before the Mineshaft closed in 1985, before its slings and bath tubs and toilets disappeared into history, Wally gave permission to the heavy-duty S&M group, The Skulls of Akron, led by filmmaker Dave Masur, to come into the Shaft and, with very primitive video equipment, make an amazing handballing tape titled *Fisting Ballet*. While finally revealing on screen (and for history) the closed set of the Mineshaft interior itself, the underground tape featured a shaved nude man climbing posts and beams above the heads of some Mineshaft rats (regulars). He hangs from pipes, lowering himself, and his wind-tunnel asshole down on the untiring arm of badman Biker Rick who always proved the most incredible REAL TOP in the whole series of S&M documentary videos made by The Skulls of Akron. The Skulls' fisting, fringe, and S&M videos disappeared through various kinds of censorship at the same time Robert Mapplethorpe's photography underwent Federal investigation in 1989.

WHY SOCIETY OWES GAYS APOLOGIES AND CASH REPARATIONS

In precisely this way, straights make legitimate records of gay history illegitimately disappear! Call your Congress person now—you are reading it here first—and demand 1) apologies and 2) cash payments to gays and lesbians for personal abuse, illegal laws, civil rights abuse, and systematic destruction of lesbigay culture's writings, images (still and moving picture), and meeting places (bars, baths, churches, etc.)

The point is: much of your normal gay life is illegal. Suddenly with the turn of the century, fisting is everywhere in video. Surprising, because fisting *per se* has been very forbidden on screen, in photos, and as a penetration act itself in the whole world, except in Amsterdam, and in 20-some States in the U.S. Thinking about buying any gay DVD (fisting or not)? Always buy DVDs and magazines when you have the chance. Censorship historically always takes your gay culture away. If you enjoy the high-tech fisting DVDs, say, of Steven Scarborough's Hot House, build your collection while you can.

FIRST-FIST INITIATION

Q. How do gay men learn? A. From each other.

On May 14, 1970, my first night as an adult in San Francisco, two very handsome men invited my lover, David Sparrow, and me out of the Tool Box bar, the Fister's Paradise created in 1963 by legendary artist and fister, Chuck Arnett who introduced the IV needle to Folsom Street leather culture. (See *Leatherfolk* book and *Life* magazine, June 26, 1964—almost five years to the day before Stonewall, June 29, 1969.) We went to their apartment two or three doors up 17th Street from the "Corner of It All" at Market and Castro. They hit on David and me because we were new kids in town, fresh faces, fresh meat, and fresh fingers/knuckles/fists/wrists. *Oooo, baby!* In what seemed like five minutes, David and I were faced by these two handsome men's four cheeks, kneeling on their knees, butts puckering, inviting, eager.

"It winked at me," David whispered.

We looked at each other. We looked at our hands that the two men had coated with thick globs of Crisco. We had just fallen off the turnip truck. We bounced a reality-check look at each other, smiled like *should we* or *shouldn't we*, then shrugged like we'd been invited to the center ring of the Big Top.

In the 1970's, all gay sex was new sex. Every night something original, unique, bizarre was revealed. There were no gay magazines *per se*. Gay journalism had yet to invent itself. Everything gay men learned was by 1) oral tradition or by 2) actual hands-on instruction. Most advice involved breaking straight (and gay) taboos about sex thoughts and erotic actions. Meditation: *If straight sex is powerful enough to change virgins, then what is the outlaw power of change in actual gay sex? One act of gay sex can make your straight reputation gay. A million acts of hetero sex can never make your gay reputation straight. So what then is the actual transforming power of Fringe Sex?*

In 1968, before Stonewall, natural gay sex drives were defined in both straight and queer pre-lib culture as anti-social behavior. What seems natural in the 21st century to a man born gay, once seemed unnatural, criminal, arrest-able stuff. Think of Oscar Wilde and Saint Genet as well as John Rechy's *Sexual Outlaw* (1977). Unenlightened straights put "deviates" away into prisons and mental hospitals where many gay men—who were being and doing only what came naturally—did a stretch as late as the 1950's and early 60's, in straight-jackets and padded restraints, shackled and handcuffed in padded cells, gagged, left in their own waste, with breaks for electro-shock. (Don't go there, dawg. You'll jerk off to everything!).

David Sparrow and I had never even heard of fisting, but we had natural erotic desires we wanted to express. We were devoutly interested in expanding our erotic repertoire westward, having played for a couple years in New York with Super Tops like Don Morrison, the rollerball roller-skate champ, and with leather photographer Lou Thomas, co-founder of Colt, who split to start the darker side of Colt, Target Studios. We had come to San Francisco to be initiated into gay sex, hippie drugs, and "California consciousness." Yeah. Sure. Whatever gets you laid. In fact, we had driven our U-Haul from conservative Chicago where guys who actually fucked butt were accused of "browning." Eek! "Don't have sex with them. They're browners!" Imagine what those shy Chi boys would have thought of fisting! That "attitude" changed with the glorious bloom of 1970's sex to liberate gay men from their inner attitudes about themselves and about male/male sex codes. Suddenly, gay men understood the pierced pecs/nipples of "the Sundance Ritual,"sometimes with fist inserted, as one of the defining acts of manhood.

THE "RAISIN" OR THE "ROSE": PUCKER UP!

"Honey," I said to myself when the 1970's crashed, "even after the Fall of Rome, you never apologize for the glory that was the Roman Empire." People, who deny the infinite good the 70's Golden Age of Liberation actually accomplished, are victims of the 80's rise—and 90's fascism—of the Marxist left-wing known as the "Politically Correct" who have done more actual harm to the lesbigay world than any right-wing fundamentalist preacher ever. The fundamentalist PC world hates Mapplethorpe, gay men's mags/videos/art, fisting, and men who read porno as much as any right-wing senator whose "Politically Corrupt" campaigns are funded by any tobacco state in the South. *Come on, people!* Say it slow: "Communism and Marxism didn't work. They officially ended when the Berlin Wall came down in November 1989!" If you depended on a Marxist commune to get you fistfucked, your ass would be a raisin, not a rose. They'd still be sitting in a circle discussing how to fist you "correctly" while singing their millionth chorus of *Kumbaya*.

THE AWAKENING

Meanwhile, back at that first night in San Francisco, coached by two experts, David and I dived into two butts that blew our minds. The feel of hot warm flesh gloving our hands, sleeving our arms, turned on a crystal clear light I never want to forget, because the first time of anything erotic, especially of handballing, focuses the senses and through them the mind in ways that is everything from real physical revelation to actual intellectual, psychic, and spiritual transfiguration. Fisting was the third time that I saw gay sex could be something mystical, transcendent, sublime. The second lesson had been bondage. The first lesson had come when we all learned to play our nipples. All of it, of course, was leather. All of it was S&M.

GLOVE SIZE MEASURES MAN

David Sparrow, a great show of a young leatherman at 24, 6' 2", and 190 furry nonfat pounds upholstered with powerful brown-red hair and freckles, had a glove size of 10. My glove size was 8.5. We were perfect lovers for eight years (and imperfect for two more years), and the pair of us, goateed, were maybe absolutely perfect that night for our hosts. They called out the Fister's chant: *"In. Easy. Okay. Back out a little. Now in. Turn 180 degrees. In. Slow. In. Yes. More. More. MORE!"*

That basic Gregorian chant, straight from the guts of monks ancient and medieval and modern and extra-terrestrial, has never changed. David and I switched butts. I felt where his size-10 hand had pushed deep into the first chamber of the ravenous hole: a velvet goldmine, wet, sucking, come alive like the Asshole of Frankenstein.

"It's ALIVE. It's ALIVE!"

(Good sex is always comedy. Ask any leather guru running a demonstration.)

The room spun with the glow flooding in from the street lights, spun from the screeching rhythms of Creedence and Janis and Jimi turning on the big reels of the tape deck, and spun still more from the primal animal cries of the two men, who had turned dervish, spinning 360 degrees on our fists. Like Linda Blair. Suddenly David jumped up, needed to go pee. The man he was servicing turned and looked at me and winked. He wanted more fist in his hungry hole. The idea was thrilling: fisting two guys at once. I slid in, worked them in unison. *First chamber. Turn. Second chamber. Slide.* One energy driving two other beings, feeling the absolute thrill, the total energy rush, of penetrating two men at once—of being inside two other beings at once. Suddenly I realized I was not fisting them. I was caught in a suctioning twin vortex of double Butt Tornado. My elbows were disappearing. I jammed the soles of my boots into the floor searching for traction so I wouldn't get snapped like a wishbone!

They were pulling me in to them, into their ass-puckers, hoovering my fingers, knuckles, wrists, forearms, and elbows into them. They were hot, wet, deep, carnivorous flowers of rosy flesh. I could feel both their hearts beating together. I was not in control. They were. They rode up my arms *whoopyteeyiyo*! It was wild, erotic, and very personal among the three of us. Going "in" through the "out" door made this the most personal of revolutionary sexual encounters. I may not have remembered their names at that moment, but in the triangulated force field of the three of us, I knew everything about them and quite a cosmic lot more about myself.

We slowed to a break, because they didn't want to cum yet. I went to check on David, who had not returned. I found him kneeling in the bathroom gagging over the toilet.

"What's the matter?" I touched his face. "Are you okay?"

He looked at me and said, "I'm okay. I'll get used to it. I could feel his heart beating."

"I could too."

"I feel like an Aztec."

"This is why we came to San Francisco."

"This," he said, "is how you leave your heart in San Francisco."

FUCK THE SHIT OUT OF HIM!

Big David Sparrow and his size-10 hands, with freckles, quickly became a popular handballing top. Rarely a fisting bottom himself, David, like so many men in the Experimental 70's, left no taboo untried. He dared open all the forbidden mysteries of ancient cults. As a top, he sniffed out the scatology factor, which, frankly, at the first, for many was an extra added attraction of handballing. Maybe it was a necessary phase of toilet training in the infancy of liberated gay identity. In the Great Gay Bermuda Triangle, NY/LA/SF, John Waters and Divine were not the only ones playing "scratch and sniff."

Edge-players reached up inside a handsome man who had not cleaned out, so they could literally handfuck the shit out of him. Check out the scatological/ fist/fetish art work of "Scat Master" Martin of Holland or the solid fist-and-toilet drawings the legendary Chuck Arnett made for the Red Star Saloon and the Ambush. There is no denying this symbiotic appeal of fisting and caca. Breaking the taboo of the fist demanded iconoclasm of all other S&M taboos.

See the "meditation" I wrote for the Arthur Tress photograph in *Drummer* 25, June 1979, existentially titled "Confession de Kafka Caca." Check as well my review of the 1977 book, *End Product: The First Taboo*, by Dan Sabbath and Mandell Hall, Preface by Abby Rockefeller, Urizen Books, New York, *Drummer* #22, May 1978. Way back then, writing what would be censored now, I exposed the DNA of S&M Culture in *Drummer* when that mag was great and golden and tuned true in writing and graphics to what its readers/

players actually were about and wanted to know. In late 1979, when *Drummer* began self-censoring to please the Pentecostal printer, Mark Hemry and I moved the raw fringe edge-play stuff to *Drummer*'s underground stepson, *Man2Man Quarterly*, the first zine of the 1980's.

DIRTY DANCING

So what, if in this millennium you actually like some of the primal scat contact and douching required by fisting etiquette and safety. From 1972-1982, satyr Thom Morrison hosted dirty-fisting parties at his edgy San Francisco house, which drew an international elite of wealth, power, and talent into fisting and coprophagy. One of the most talented, Gerhardt Poule, was art director of a prestigious German magazine. In 1976, he shot the first commercial-grade, but very private, 8mm films of fisting and scat. I first viewed the footage when David Sparrow sent along Gerhardt with his Technicolor reels to *Drummer*. Even though I was creating an archetypal fetish identity for *Drummer*, even very-lib Gay Lib was not ready for the gay world's second best-kept secret. (The first best-kept secret was the IV needle—used for shooting speed and steroids.) *Drummer* turned many fringe fetishes mainstream, publishing the world's first mainstream FFA articles (Fist Fuckers of America) and first fist-related photographs along with articles on TT, VA, S&M, WS, BD, CBT, CP, SCAT and other sex-coded secrets.

COMING OUT: ONCE! TWICE!

First: The historical point of "coming out" is "coming out" *personally* to what turns YOU on. Second: You "come out" to confront the totems/taboos of society, because totems and taboos by their reflexive nature usually repress personality. (*Personally Correct* is the opposite of *Politically Correct*.) What is "coming out" if it's not the "coming out" to be the person you are, doing what you really prefer and like. As a sex analyst, I wrote originally in 1977 in *Drummer* that men have a "First Coming Out" into sex, and then, surprise, a "Second Coming Out" into kinky sex. In 1972, S&M needed a wider definition which I conceptualized to mean "Sensual" and "Mutual" to free it from the selfish polarities of Top and Bottom. Every year the evolution of Fringe Sex into manners, psychology, and spirituality requires new key word vocabulary.

As a journalist, I approached every "coming out" S&M Fringe Secret with a gonzo eye, participatory (to a point), figuring that what gay culture wanted to know must be written about, photographed, and published if gay culture were ever going to "come out" from the middle ages of the Eisenhower 50's and the early 60's, before assassination, the Beatles, and Hippies changed everything. Only in the Stonewall Year of 1969 did the U.S. Postal Department finally make it legal to show frontal male nudity. This victory against the Fig Leaf of government censorship created the New Heart of gay publishing, and, therefore, gay culture. The champions who fought the good fight were Chuck Renslow, the leather/muscle mogul of Chicago, and Bob Mizer, the Hollywood genius behind *Physique Pictorial* magazine and AMG movies. Check out *PP*'s coded hieroglyph drawings revealing the secret sex tastes of the models of Mizer's Athletic Model Guild/AMG Studios. (*Hieroglyph* means literally "sacred, holy, consecrated writing.")

STEVE'S OWN PRIVATE CATACOMBS

On May 5, 1975, the Irish-American Catholic Steve McEachern founded his own private "Catacombs." (I still have my invitation to the opening orgy!) The name, *Catacombs*, was a pointedly religious term, spun sarcastically, to reflect the Catholic cultural roots of sexual "transubstantiation" through fisting and S&M fringe sex. Steve made the basement of his Victorian on 21st Street the hottest "invitation only" party in the world. If Steve didn't personally know you, then you had to know somebody who knew somebody. His fisting buddies were his lover, Michael Shapley, who had moved to San Francisco in the Fall of 1973; his master of ceremonies, George Delaney, a tall rogue Irishman from Chicago—where in 1968, George cruising had picked me up sunbathing in Grant Park; and his mentor, Tony Tavarossi, the legendary sex guru born in San Francisco's Mission district. My 1977 interview with Steve McEachern was published in *Drummer* 23 (July 1978) because to know the daily life of the past is as important to one's future as to know how physical sex is the gateway to the stars. Moving into the 21st century, beginners can check conveniently into whatever Gay Chat Room and find a community dying to tell them everything. In the 70's, it was every man for himself. Hands-on Adventure was king.

FRENCH-FRIED FRINGE: FISTING FOUCAULT

Serious students of S&M can also thumb through the writings of the French philosopher, Michel Foucault (1926-1984). Edge-Player Foucault lived a magical mystery tour. He polished quite a bit of his transforming philosophy in the 70's and early 80's during his Nietzschean Fringe Play on his knees, fisted, South of Market, at the Cauldron, the Slot, and other clubs where S&M, torture, piss, scat, and, *mai oui*, fisting taught him everything he knew about polymorphous perversions that transform the Tribe of Queer Boys through dramatic extremities of Fringe Sex. Think about this eyewitness Queer History: somebody had to fist Foucault and torture him, and I can tell you that those ooh-la-la services came out of the salon circling my editing desk at *Drummer*. (What's more droll than fisting the French?) If the strip-shaved X-treme Foucault could have starred in Pasolini's Fascist sex fantasy, *Salo*, he would have, but then, seeking the sexual transcendence of the Marquis de Sade himself, wouldn't we all?

S&M PLAYERS BEGIN INCESTUOUSLY

A few days after our virginal first night of fisting, one of our hosts, who, of course, turned out to be Steve McEachern, introduced David Sparrow and me to Walter Jebe, who owned the first camera shop in the 60's in the Castro, long before Harvey Milk blew into town to Manhattanize San Francisco. In July 1970, Walt Jebe hired the pair of us as leather S&M models for two black-and-white shoots of 200-300 photographs, which were turned into one of the first 1-issue leather magazines, *Whipcrack* (1971). When publisher John Embry hired me as his founding San Francisco editor-in-chief of *Drummer*, I brought—again the pair of us—David Sparrow along as photographer. Under the names "Spitting Image" and "David A. Sparrow," we together shot most of the photographs in *Drummer* issues 20-30, including my design of the first-ever Fisting Cover which appeared on *Drummer* 30, featuring in color Val Martin and Bob Hyslop, who both modeled for Jim French at Colt, Lou Thomas at Target, Mikal Bales at Zeus, and me at Palm Drive Video. In one degree of fringe separation, I also hired Steve McEachern, who ran his transcribing business from his living room above the Catacombs. Steve did the transcribing of all my interviews for *Drummer*, which was the third magazine founded after Stonewall. Actually, this fact is epicentric to queer history: every masculine-identified gay male magazine that followed owes its identity, erotic themes, and fetish culture to the "Daddy of All Leather/Power Journalism," *Drummer* itself, which—I will be the first to say—became an entity bigger than any editor, writer, photographer, artist, or publisher.

LEATHER S&M ARCHETYPES: GENOME AS DESTINY

In the human genome of 80,000 genes, we are all so alike (99.9% of genes) that there is only 1 in 1,000 genome letters' difference between Woody Allen and Arnold Schwarzenegger and you. You have the genome of S&M naturally. Also, what allows you to be an S&M Leather Player reading about S&M has a long bright cultural history. Your heritage goes back many years to a throng of players who yanked gay power from our endorphin-enriched bodies. They saw our bodies as temples. They jacked physical sex up into art, politics, and erotic freedom. Sex has become a valid kind of spiritual self-actualization. Actually, your history testifies you're not just a cocksucker or fistfucker or whipmeister. Your Freudian gay sex DNA has a Jungian archetypal identity. It creates you, aura and being, through your erotic stimulation. Robert Mapplethorpe told me, "Intelligent sex is the best sex." Geoff Mains, author of *Urban Aboriginals*, said, "Intuitive sex leads to joy." Michael Rosen wrote, "S&M is Sex Magic." Sex can make you a human being with a soul. Read Walt Whitman's *Song of Myself*, which is one tradition of homosex: the sunny Billy Budd. The other is the dark existential French tradition of homosex from Rimbaud: Captain Vere who ties up and hangs Billy Budd.

If you are young, you're lucky—even though you missed the 1970's. Before you were born, men experiencing fists and S&M began thinking about fisting and S&M, creating prose and art and photography and films of fisting and S&M. Even though some people say fisting isn't S&M, it's still a debate. The truth is you live in a fully realized fist-and-S&M culture of advice (spelled this way) and consent that is its own best invention.

SOMEBODY HAS TO DO THE PAPERWORK

Highly recommended for men interested in the concept "Where Fringe Sex Came From" is former *Advocate*-editor Mark Thompson's brilliantly eclectic *Leatherfolk: Radical Sex, People, Politics, and Practice*, Alyson Press, 1991.

You'll learn the names of S&M Fringe Pioneers like biker-bear Geoff Mains (*Urban Aboriginals*); artist Chuck Arnett; GMSMA's historian, David Stein; former *Drummer* and Brush Creek editor, Joseph W. Bean; university professor, Dr. Gayle Rubin (detailed, human history of the Catacombs); my mentor and longtime friend, Sam Steward; prison bondage guru Harold Cox; the gent and scholar, Patrick Califia; the loincloth androgyne, Purusha, who liked my premise that homosexuality is an ancient religion older than Pagans, Druids, Judaism, Christianity, and Islam; fisting entrepreneur Steve McEachern; psychotherapist Guy Baldwin; and the Monk of True North, Fakir Musafar, who shows us all what mystic transcendence is really all about; and many others who have contributed to the culture of sexual self-realization, and transformative body chemistry, particularly through the endgame culture of the fist.

As a self-actualizing gonzo journalist, Mark Thompson, who also wrote *Gay Spirit: Myth and Meaning*, has de-programmed the once popular mid-70's *Advocate*-version of Werner Erhard's EST. (Mark Thompson was one of the most significant editors of *The Advocate*.) Once quite S&M virginal, the genial genius Thompson has dared extend himself intellectually into actual physical scenes that have sophisticated his transformative writing. I mention him in *Popular Witchcraft*, because while not traditional "Trad Leather," he has incorporated Christian, pagan, new age, and Native American wisdom into the gay faerie cosmic mix. His gonzo journey seems seeded with reflexive ideas from his longtime life partner, the priest, Father Malcolm Boyd, who wrote the best-seller, *Are You Running with Me, Jesus?* To which we always irreverently added: "...*Or Just Breathing Hard?*"

At first, S&M, fisting, scat, and drugs were, like venereal disease and death, verboten/forbidden topics even in the rebellious, newly-founded gay press. Times change people. Queers never used to die, except as suicides at the end of novels, films, and plays. Death was so unnatural to the gay psyche that it was a taboo subject. For a long time. Until Harvey Milk's assassination. Until AIDS obituaries. Until the cafes of empty chairs and empty tables.

Death itself turned fisting around. Many handballers died fast in huge numbers as the Plague passed over some houses and killed in other houses it did not pass over. These deaths-by-virus caused many passed-over handballers to tune into something, well, cosmic, spiritual, mystical, and very, very physical. Early on, the morning after Stonewall, it truly was the "Dawning of the Age of Aquarius." But then...who knew? Who ever knows? We're all on a flight over Locherbie anyway, so we might as well get fisted in the Mile-High First-Class Toilet.

"It wasn't fisting what done 'em in. It wasn't sex what killed 'em. It was the needle. It was intravenous drugs." Never go there.

DIRTY NEEDLES

The most beautiful people, the "Hot Men," the "A-Group" models and film stars of that first generation of fisters were all hoisted on their own petards (needles) and swept from the streets of San Francisco, LA, and New York. Newsflash: Men had died of undiagnosed HIV in the mid-70's. The AIDS "look," then not yet identified, usually sent them back to the towns and families they came from. They disappeared from the gay radar, because illness—except for amoeba cocktails of Flagel—was considered the least tasteful thing a gay man could do during the world-wide orgy. Actually, I think one of the reasons I survived the 70's was because my doctor, Fred Hudson, gave me gamma globulin shots every six weeks to survive the then known erotic dangers.

Quitting drugs. That was spiritually the best thing that happened to S&M and handballing, because without drugs masking sensation, actual sensation became approachable through erotic hypnosis, zen meditation, tantric tactics, and mutual conversations of deep TRUST between top and bottom.

Robert Frost wrote about "building *stone walls*" that we learn from our hands to our head. He means you can't understand something in your head unless it's brought to your unclouded brain through your hands, that is, your physical body. So it is that we learn from our sexual bodies to our heads and spirits and souls.

FROM HERE TO FRATERNITY

"Leather stands apart," my pal Geoff Mains writes, "in exploring sexual capacities in terms of ecstatic experience. To its participants, leather sex [such as fisting] brings release and revelation. And to the world, leather becomes at once a symbol and a culture. A black and animal side of the soul has been rediscovered and let out." — "The Molecular Anatomy of Leather" in *Leatherfolk*; see also Geoff Mains, *Urban Aboriginals: A Celebration of Leather Sexuality*, Gay Sunshine Press, San Francisco, 1984. Mains, a scientist, presaged with his molecular theory the current genome theory. Brilliant!

In the S&M short fiction anthology, *Rainbow County*, "Peter Eton-Cox, hanging bound upside down, wearing only black leather chaps and boots, had never felt his body to be more of a sacred vessel than at this whipping. If grace existed in the universe, then he was hanging suspended and open to the flow. The harder the Cowboys whipped him, the less nay-saying he felt, until transcended beyond all negativity, on the edge of Total *Yes*, he heard the crack of the bullwhip across the barn....Peter no longer cared about dick. This game had progressed beyond genital sex. He wondered which whiplash had taken the energy from his dick and shot it to his head. Maybe it was endorphins. Maybe it was God. He knew the Cowboys had dared to go beyond games, turning his body into a medium for conjuring something so raw and primitive it had no name....They had left civilization now....This rush defined *rush*....He didn't know if he wanted more whipping or not. Cowboy Dogg Katz was a legend. This moment might never come again. He sensed it. He embraced it. He loved himself, yeah, finally, and he loved these men, whoever they really were, and he loved this whiphand Dogg Katz more than he had ever loved or felt anything in his life.

"...The bullwhip cracked and sang louder, faster, heavier. Peter felt everything. He felt nothing. He was inside himself. He was outside himself. He was one with them. He could feel the energy of the Whiphand Cowboy, Dogg Katz, flowing down into him. His blood ran down his back toward his shoulders. The clock stopped. He was screaming. The clock was running backwards. He was in ecstasy. The clock melted down. His body was quivering. The men were untying him, taking him down, lowering him, laying him flat out on the floor, standing him up to see their work on his butt, walking him to the mattress, all hands laying him back, sitting together with him, and him with them, and all of them together....The bullwhip had opened him up: head and body. There was no resistance left in him. Even if they had taken him out to the four-holer outhouse, where men were kept tied to bondage boards in the cesspit in the broiling desert heat, he would not have objected....Dogg Katz, licking his lips, was greasing up his fist." –From "S&M Ranch" by Jack Fritscher, reprinted from *MAN2MAN* #2, December 1980, and *Powerplay* #19, 1998; also appears in a slightly different version in *Some Dance to Remember: A Memoir-Novel of San Francisco 1970-1982* (1990, new edition 2005); based on a 1978 scene at the Barracks conducted and produced by Top Shaman, Peter Fiske, Whipmeister.

WHEN DISCO MET CRISCO IN FRISCO

Handballing is an exercise in "learning to let go" of what we perceive to be the primary point of control. Our butts. The anus is so *way* protected. Straight men's biggest fear is anal penetration. Understand why Marines tattoo their butts with "Death before Dishonor." Fisting connects radically—by its roots—not only to scatology but to other S&M Fringe Sex like bondage and Extreme Tits.

Initially, bondage preceded fisting. Ropes heightened focus. Leather controlled wild movements of a bottom-in-training. Bondage of yet-flexible wrists, ankles, and torso is the underlying concept of the "SLING" which at first was invented for S&M torture and for ease of butt penetration by a topfucker's dick. In a sling, the bottom's body transcends gravity. *Push cums to shove.* A fist — "Simple logic, Captain"— becomes an inevitability. A w/hole new world opens up!

By spring 1975, the handballing sling officially had entered gay culture through two legendary fisting pits: the Catacombs and the Slot Hotel, a "bath" South of Market. The Barracks, on Folsom at Hallam Mews, was fronted by Chuck Arnett's fisty Red Dog Saloon. The Barracks was the A-List's #1 hot-sex bath where *acid + orgy combined* in early 1972 to change the face of polite suck/fuck sex forever, particularly with rooms dedicated to S&M and fisting. The acid jug, like bathtub gin in an office water cooler, stood in a pot in the lobby. "Drink the Kool-Aid!" One leather player one night dressed himself up in a French maid's little black uniform and walked up and down the Barracks halls with a feather duster asking anyone and everyone if they wanted "to get dusted." He created a laugh sensation because the drug of choice that season was angel dust. The Barracks got so hot, the crowd boiled over to the fist-focused Slot which could have used a French maid to clean up. Finally, the Barracks got so ultra hot it burned up in licks of flame in August 1981, about the same time Steve McEachern, quite famously (and if I know Steve, quite loaded) checked out with a heart attack impaled on the arm of his lover in a private scene at the Catacombs. Rest in peace, old son!

SLOT SoMa: *EROTIC HANDS*, FIRST FISTING MOVIE

In this way, the former blue-collar hotel, the Slot, 979 Folsom, South of Market, was the place where S&M and fisting broke out of men's own homes into a successful and very accommodating environment. The sexy hired help cleaned up the mess after you and your 13 partners went home smelling of beer, pot, tobacco, poppers, shit, piss, and Crisco. And that was just the air! A square inch of the hall carpet at the Slot could have caused any plague, but the Slot was slag hot! Even if you didn't use drugs. The Slot's great blue poster promised three floors of hot guys/hot fists/hot butts.

On more than one night you could share some handshaking time with each one of the three-man cast of the first fisting film, the classic 1976 Technicolor epic, *Erotic Hands*, starring Richard Trask, a hot blond named Billy, and a third guy, a co-star with a beard who liked to give you plenty of elbow room...but, wow, that's another story of the glorious Slot, where the coolest of the cool every year booked rooms for all national holidays—particularly New Year's Eve—to date the international talent trawling the hallways all the way from Manhattan, Berlin, Amsterdam, Paris, and Algeria. My room, which I used about 104 nights a year for at least five years was 326, first room on the left, top of the stairs, third floor.

A note for collectors: Copies of vintage films and videos, such as *Erotic Hands*, as well as back issues of nearly all gay magazines including some underground zines from even before Stonewall, can be found at good prices at the store called "The Magazine," 920 Larkin, San Francisco 94109. Regarding *Erotic Hands*, all movies of gay culture before 1982 were silent films. Two pioneering exceptions: J. Brian made the first gay talkie, *Four More Than Money* (1971), based on the Sam Steward (Phil Andros) leather autobiography, *Stud* (1966); Derek Jarman used sound for his S&M epic *Sebastiane* (1976) - whose dialogue was all in Latin - long before Mel Gibson's wet S&M epic *Passion of the Christ*. Video arrived almost at the same time as HIV. I had to explain this once to a very young film student who *demanded* I show her my videotapes of the Stonewall rebellion for her college Communication Arts course! Some people think the world began the day they began to notice it.

TONY TAVAROSSI: THE S&M LORD OF THE FIST

At the Slot, in 1975, with the Slot's cooperation, I shot in Room 226, first door at the left of the stairs, second floor, in the room with stocks, three silent reels of fisting movies, with heavy bondage. My Super-8 Technicolor epic starred the best and first fister in San Francisco, Tony Tavarossi. That was the official film start of what became Palm Drive Video. (Palm Drive is an erotic pun, not a street address.) Tony Tavarossi, "The S&M Lord of the Fist," grew up in the Mission. He came out at age twelve under the tables of the South China Café at 18th and Castro. (Go there for sweet and sour on your next pilgrimage to SFO.) During my twelve-year friendship with Tony, he told me he was first fistfucked in 1957 by a sailor in an Oceanside motel while hanging upside down, tied by his feet to the showerhead. Tony was an ethnic Italian who literally invented the red-light-and-black-paint ambience of the leather bars in New York (specifically, the Anvil), and San Francisco, including Chuck Arnett's Tool Box. He worked at the Barracks, managed the Slot, and was always the Guest of Honor at the Catacombs.

On the Panhandle to Golden Gate Park, Tony had equipped his own apartment with a sling, a douche bath with bondage, music, and the most inventive ass and tit torture toys this side of heaven. Tony said he was "a slave born to serve masters who needed some balance from always being tops." (Examine that line! That's how clever he was at getting exactly what he wanted.) Tony was a god—he looked like the satyr Pan, and I pray to him to this day. The world beat a path to his fist in his S&M harem. All he asked in return from any man was an affectionate fist once in awhile. In August 1981, in the ICU of San Francisco General, I held his sweet hand. I told him that the Barracks had burned down two nights before. He could not speak, but he wrote: "Good." I asked the doctor, "What's wrong with him?" She said, "We don't know. We've never seen a patient so distressed." Tony died the next day. Again, it wasn't the fisting; it was the needle. Everyone in San Francisco arrived at his huge funeral. No one of us had ever really died in 1981. But Tony couldn't go away to another town to die. He was born at San Francisco General. At his huge funeral, every top in town got to see every other top who had secretly bottomed to Tony Tavarossi's Lordly Fist!

EINE KLEINE FIST MUSIK

By 1976, the Handball Express baths, 975 Harrison, and the Waiting Arms International Hotel, 1188 Folsom, and the Mineshaft in New York, and Man Space in Los Angeles cashed in on the rage of fisting, the new religion buzzed by rhythms of drug-and-fist anthems. Singer Grace Slick drove the "Bolero" out of "White Rabbit." Red-hot guitarist Tim Buckley sang virtually about the open w/holiness of butthole-to-fist in "Sweet, Sweet Surrender." Grace Jones ruled the night with "*La Vie en Rose.*" The soundtrack at the baths was an incredible tape mix of albums created by several different DJs. Prime among them in taste and popularity, and always the first with the newest, was shit-fister Thom Morrison who, even while he was my pal for more than fourteen years, was mysteriously "connected" to the underworld of music producers. (Don't ask; I didn't.) Music drove fisting up to a higher level. Disco *per se* finally became a joke among leatherfolk , but at first it was as "hot, cool, and in" as anything is at any given time. Addicted to the rhythm, many a gay man gladly gave up his fist-hole while a gorgeous black woman, singing conjure-*obeah*, clued him—the way Grace Jones clued us all—into what it was to really, Really, REALLY "need a man." The Pointer Sisters sang the bottom line of fisting: "I want a man with a slow hand, I want a lover with an easy touch."

Tennessee Williams wrote, "Suddenly there's God so quickly." Tenn could have been describing what men learned in late nights of fisting when, handballed into ecstasy, they saw down into the sacred "Tunnel of Purple Poppered Divine Light," even though they knew nothing about tantric yoga, energy chakras, or how monks in the Middle Ages achieved mysticism through disciplines of fasting, scourging, sleep deprivation, and fisting. "You say *Apollo*. I say *Dionysius*. Let's call the w/hole thing off!" Like people on TV talking about their near-death experiences and how they saw the light and decided not to go, many men saw down that Purple Tunnel and decided not to go. I know.

MONK OF THE HOLY FIST: PURUSHA

In 1981, the former Benedictine monk, Peter Larkin, indulged by his wealthy parents who loved him, self-published a cornerstone book which he wrote mapping out the physical and mystical geography of fisting. The hard-bound, richly printed volume, *The Divine Androgyne*, was actually titled, *The Divine Androgyne according to Purusha: Adventures in Cosmic Erotic Ecstasy and Androgyne Bodyconsciousness* (all one word). Because in 1981 there were no gay book publishers to actually print books, especially a cult book about fisting, Peter Larkin created Sanctuary Publications named for his San Diego Sanctuary of men pursuing spiritual enlightenment through a brotherhood of fisting, meditation, discipline, piercing, tattoos, as well as study of Christian and Asian theology. He lavishly illustrated the gospel of his words in *The Divine Androgyne* with his art, paintings, and photographs.

In 1981, I was able to interview Purusha and experience his earthy presence. As a former seminarian myself, having spent eleven years directly subject to the pope in Rome at the Pontifical College Josephinum, I was formally trained in theology and familiar with the writings of mystics and monks and the Fathers of the Church. Peter Larkin liked our similar background, and I found him as "Purusha," to be well within the global mainstream of spiritual enlightenment in both his intellectual thought *and* his physical mortification of the body which lead to genuine spiritual life.

TODAY'S HIGH: IN THE '70'S

Purusha was a spiritual pioneer at a time when A-Group fisters, like my intense pal, Colt model, Jim Graham, were inviting good FFA tops and TT tops to fly down to Los Angeles where we were then flown by helicopter some distance out into the desert to the top of snow-covered mountains. The deluxe, catered weekend, opulent as a harem in a chalet, was closed from Friday entrance to Sunday afternoon exit when the helicopters returned. The Colt-type handsome men at this prodigal mountain retreat may or may not have gotten into a *yin* mystical consciousness. They certainly got a *yang* high off the fisting, the drugs, and the partying with men so ideally masculine they could make a straight man go gay. Yet these sexual athletes, understanding the physical pleasure of fisting, were not so far a cry from Purusha's balanced *yinyang* Sanctuary of pierced, fisted men in San Diego, where drugs were a more integrated part of training the w/hole person.

Frankly, it is impossible to discuss fisting without mentioning drugs: Midol to crystal methamphetamine. Only in the mid-80's did drug-free fisting, like drug-free bodybuilding, become like, uh, a reality. Mmmm, yeah, whatever.

THE NEW UNREPRESSED, UNCLOSETED SELF

Time has proven Purusha to be one of the Pioneer Patron Saints of Male Ecstasy. Born near St. Louis, he had the world's best education about sex. He studied literature, creative writing, philosophy, and theology at Rollins College in Florida. He then spent ten years in Roman Catholic monastic life, first with the Congregation of Holy Cross at Notre Dame, Indiana, and then as a Benedictine monk at Saint Bernard Abbey in Alabama and Mount Savior Monastery in New York. He earned a BA in philosophy from Notre Dame University, and a Master of Arts in theology from Saint Michael's College in the University of Toronto. He was a religious counselor at Yale University, and in 1974 produced, co-authored, and directed one of the first feature movies of gay liberation to go mainstream on theater screens, *A Very Natural Thing*, which, as a DVD rental at Netflix, may give an easier introduction to Purusha's head space than diving first thing into his book.

He early on picked up on the "closeted spirituality" inherent in gay culture. Ultimately, for everyone, "uncloseted gay spirit" arose through sex...and, for some, through priest-shaman drugs used in the anthropological *yin* fashion of cultures alternative to American male *yang* consciousness.

Purusha said, "About my new unrepressed self, I can only say that it emerges inside me, blooms inside me, each minute, hour, day and night. The unrepressed me feels like a new me, reawakened, more original, natural, primitive, mythic. I can now fall in love with my self the way I once fell so in love with strangers, and that way I can love these other strangers all the more....I look for the taboos in American culture and I try to break them to free myself from them and awaken my body, my full eroticism, my real feelings and true emotion so I can respond to Nature Itself and to the Universe Itself as I find the Universal Nature *within* myself and *within* other men. That is why I invite like-minded men to my Sanctuary."

Purusha's Chapter 4 is the heart of his book. Its title reveals its guts: "Advanced Male Androgyne: Eroticism and Tantra—1) Psycho-Sexual Androgyny, 2) Erotic Pain and Piercing, 3) Fistfucking: Yoga of Cosmic Erotic Ecstasy." If you're gay, you don't need to live in the new-age town of "Granola, California," to figure out there's a deep message here to those who have ears to hear and eyes to see and butts to fist. Actually, to both Old School and New School BDSM players *The Divine Androgyne* may be an informative guide to anyone pursuing the meaning, the sensuality, and the spirituality of bodies and minds.

THE ART OF THE FIST

The cover of *The Divine Androgyne* is a very sexy color drawing of thirteen multicultural men each one fisting the other arranged in a daisy-chain circle of fist-up-butt to fist-up-another-butt, until all thirteen, like Christ and the twelve Apostles, are connected, fisted *and* fisting in a perfect energy circle. This original Sanctuary mandala was drawn by Purusha and then illustrated by Robert Uyvari for the cover as well as for a very popular poster sold by Los Angeles' Eons Gallery. Eons also represented original Tom of Finland on his first trip to the US in 1977, as well as the Leathermaster, Fistmaster, Bearmaster drawings by Jakal, another artist/player obsessed with the fantasy arms and fists of godlike Fisting Tops.

The peerless L.A. artist and FFA Top, Skipper, who began life as a Laguna surfer, has drawn many gutsy fisting fantasy pictures of which one of his best is "Football Fisting." Check his work at Greasetank.com. Skipper draws driven by operatic masturbation. He cums only when the drawing is finished. Or vice versa. What kind of artists give you that kind of focused energy! When you look at any of these fisting images, stare at them till your eyes cross and you fall into the frame and feel the powerful mystique all these artists draw from their actual handballing experience into images created by their fisting hands.

QUEER CULTURE: GENDER OF A FIST

Just as feminists can theorize legitimately about homofemininity, all these artists and photographers emphasize the manly homomasculinity inherent in the ritual of fisting. In these days of gender equality, fisting seems to remain its own original recipe. In fact, in these days when many kinky straight people run classified ads in gay mags, because our gay culture is so open to everyone, and we provide the only base where they might find partners matching their kink, one must consider the nature of kinky partnering across gender.

For instance, women advertising they want to fist men are setting up a straight scene; kinky, yes, but straight. If you're a man who prefers men, then consider the psychological overtones and social reality of what fisting a woman, or being fisted by a woman means. Actually, in the wisdom of the world, that's *heterosexuality*. Do you want *heterosex* in any way shape or form to get inside you? As much as I respect her person and gender, I'd rather not date Sigourney (*Alien*) Weaver! (*I'm such a homo!*) *Internal* massage? Hey! Even cross-gender *external* massage on a table short-circuits to weird hetero energy. Whatever. You decide. It's your trip. Psychotherapist Guy Baldwin writes, "A hardon is not politically correct."

Question the psychic truth of that premise. How would you define a man fisting another man? Theories of gender polarities in conjuration are so central that a reference to the book *Popular Witchcraft* saves discussing lesbian-lesbian conjurations, or male-female polarities, etc.

No one alive would call a man fisting another man anything but *homosexual* no matter how straight both men said they were. Cross-gender fisting? Anything is possible at astral levels, but let's keep it simple, literal, and cool. We can reconsider this much later, in the 22'nd century, because in the post-Bush Dynasty of 2100 A.D., everyone will be so much, uh, more enlightened.

DOES *YIN* TRUMP *YANG*?

For now, be careful psychically how you position gender in your kinky play. No gay man has ever gone straight. The transcendental point is to respect the difference of actual gender *yin* (females) from actual gender *yang* (males) in order to not confuse the psycho-erotic *yin* and the psycho-erotic *yang* combined in one person. Both strict homosexuality and strict heterosexuality are equally noble when natural to the persona. But so is, some like editor Ron Suresha say, bisexuality. Nothing trumps anything in the song of your self.

By Purusha's definition, his sense of androgyny hardly justifies effeminate males or butch females. (The fascist pig!) The DNA Genome of his "androgyne" refers only to persons interested in harmonizing their active, aggressive, rational *yang* energies with their own receptive, yielding, intuitive *yin* energies inside one human personality. Gosh! Fisting and mysticism that make you more of an integrated human inside your self. And you thought you were only having sex! What a concept!

"HELLO! TOILET TRAINING, IMPALEMENT, & TRUST. PLEASE HOLD."

Fisting has always been an exercise in learning to let go of what we perceive to be the most controllable thing in our body: our butts. As children in toilet training, once we got control of our peeing and pooping, our parents freed us up to go anywhere. To learn, Grasshopper, that the butt is *The Way Out,* is first step to learning that the butt is also *The Way In.* To learn this active passivity, even in a *mondo-sleazo* game room, is growth. To be impaled on another human male's hand/fist/arm/foot grabs your attention and yanks your focus. Impalement is a kind of bondage.

When a hand is up your rectum, you ain't going anywhere, nor do most people want to go. Handballing, like bondage, is worthwhile, the way a monk's contemplative life is worthwhile as a human lesson in will, in power, in sweet-sweet surrender of will and power, in life itself. Handball is a yoga-like *yinyang* unifying experience.

Check this out: A man breaks western taboo about the anus. He finally submits to total and complete penetration. He relaxes into it and feels it from the inside out. He even cums to the otherworldly wildness of such pleasure. He learns a radical/root lesson of cosmic discipline and cosmic truth. He detaches. He learns how to detach. He experiences how to sweetly surrender control, how to get off on the lack of control, knowing that control is not gone, but just transferred from the self to another, in trust, absolute trust.

STRONG MAN WITH A SLOW HAND

When, by sliding down a hand/wrist/arm/elbow, your body gives up the control *it thinks/you think it has/you have*, then your mind can finally begin to relax and trust. Impaled, floating in a sling, you are above gravity and out of the world, regressed to comfortable womb memories. There is no distraction. There is only your physical body, sweaty under the hot lights or steaming in candle glow. When your consciousness comes down out of your head and goes to the perfect circle of your butt, then emerges your self, your inner self, your ego. Your astral body becomes free as in sleep, but better than sleep, because your conscious mind is awake, is experiencing the other side of your self, is recording what it is to be body-made-flesh with all defenses and attitude dropped.

You drift internally, down through all the incredible movement inside your own hide (no longer living in solitary confinement in your own skin), penetrated by another being, down to the chakra of your belly, your guts (the energy center behind your navel). You begin to find your center that has nothing to do with the car you drive, or the job you have, or the rent you pay. Your center is also not in your head as you were taught, and not in your dick as you thought. Your energy is throughout your whole body. Your energy is not in your head alone. When you live in your head alone, or follow only your dick around, you become disturbed. Massage of ass-lips, prostate, colon, and chakras can bring you to your senses. You need a strong man with a slow hand deep in your Tunnel of Love!

THE MAN WHO FELL TO EARTH

Wisely, William Wordsworth said, "The world is too much with us late and soon, getting and spending." Let a trusted hand break through that world's clocks and cash. Mirrors reflect only surfaces. A mirror says that you, strangling in your tie and suit, are in control. A playroom mirror says that you, all spread out in a sling, are in control. Then the Hand-Mirror of the Inserted Fist reflects your exact place in the universe. *You are a Hand Puppet of the Universe*. You understand the spiritual *yin* of what your daily *yang* is really about. Penetrated, relaxing, surrendering, dropping all your energy out your hungry hole, you begin to learn on your sensual monk's journey that Earth is but a rest-stop with playrooms. This planet, like the house of your body, is not the end of your self's journey. Earth is a way station for your internal existential consciousness that knows deep down, right now, in this time, in this moment, in this flesh, on this planet, twirling on a fist, your real soul is about to be spun out beyond the universe!

Out-of-the-body experiences, short of hallucinogens, are rare.
Be careful what sex games you play.
Never fisted, you may live all your life not knowing
what knowledge this way comes.
Once fisted, you may experience what monks and mystics
have known for ages.
Like Adam and Eve, once you bite whatever apple you were forbidden,
you may find that you have gained knowledge you can never forget.
Drink deep or drink not at all from the energy locked up
in the ring of your ass.
Be good humored. Geoff Mains wrote that the
Patroness of Fisting is Miss Piggy.

FISTING YOUR ZYGOTE, DUDE!

Did you know that when you are a zygote, in the first moments of your conception, that the zygote is a small two-or-three-celled womb creature shaped like the letter *C*? Life's energy at this quick stage runs like electricity along the backbone of the *C*-shaped zygote trying to determine which leg of the *C* will become the mouth and which will become the anus. The lifeforce energy speeds back and forth, end to end, until nature decides which end is top and which is bottom.

You may know, as I have known, several people who in their adult life have had pains in their butt which could only be cured by having the teeth impacted around their tail bones removed. They could not floss these unknown teeth near their butt. This proves that nature can be momentarily ambiguous top to bottom. If either leg of the *C* could be the brain, then maybe you've got a Smart Ass. Like a Smart Bomb. Assplay can reveal the imbalance of being trapped up in a rational head. That zygote thing can also explain why some people can't tell their head from their ass.

Actually, if either end of your spine could be your butt or your brain, then maybe biology itself teaches we should all respect a bit more the capacity for thinking and insight that is the butt's own wisdom. The dick/nipples/balls/butt are cello strings of the body that, as a very physical instrument, can be put between the legs and played, say, through actual stroking and physical penetration and piercing, to transcend up the physical scale to metaphysical insight, to the astral way. The Romans had a saying: "*Per aspera ad astra. Through tough discipline to the stars.*"

Transcendence is the pure conjuring of the astral body of the spirit that comes in through your fleshbody, and then blooms deep inside you. If you are a man in pursuit of the pure essence of your self, varieties of sexplay, such as fisting, can help guide and teach you and introduce you to your Self.

> Trust me.
> By now I'm up to my wrist inside you.
> If you were a genetically straight male, none of this would be happening to you.
> It's your gift from the gods.

"Perhaps," as beefcake Andrew Sullivan wrote in *Virtually Normal*, "this is a homosexual privilege...the [gay] human personality begins to develop differently. (Andrew Sullivan, *Virtually Normal: An Argument about Homosexuality*, p. 92, Knopf, 1995.)

JUMP FROM GENITAL TO FULL-BODY ORGASM

Cuming, any cuming, fisted or unfisted, no matter how you get your orgasm, is the only transcendent freedom finite humans can ever know. While you're cuming, nothing matters: not rent, not food, not loved ones, not even physical life itself. Any man who has ridden his own orgasm, riding a fist the way a good cowboy rides his horse, knows that during his cuming, he could die; would, in fact, willingly die, because anything else on this planet has got to be less than this. Through fisting, whole body orgasm is achievable. In short, a man who has only felt his dick cum, could, through the liberating wisdom of fine-tuning his butthole, enjoy his whole body cuming, much the way women totally cum, but yet different from women, different in the way that men and women are analogs of each other.

So DIGITize me, Baby, with those five fingers!

The French, wise in the psychology of sex, call orgasm *la petite mort*, the little death. If there is a Heaven (and orgasm, again, by analog, suggests there must be), then Heaven, at the least, better be an eternal orgasm. If it's not, then it's just another fucking shuck, and the so-called Religious Right (not to be confused with actual Christians who worship Jesus) are welcome to it all by their loathsome lonesome.

Modern life, as we live it, mostly working, etc., is simply what you do on this planet between cumings. What we do, occupations, recreation, friends, everything, is just filler to rest on between the high energy conjurations of cumings. Orgasm is ALL, some/most feel. Too bad it doesn't last longer. Perhaps the next best thing is tantric foreplay, with the *yin* of tits and butthole, that works both longer and on a lot of levels more than the *yang* sex of wham-bam.

Perhaps it is such psychic re-wiring that best explains 21st-century men's increasing **man**stream interest in formerly fringe sex like fisting, bondage, titwork, piercing, pain, tattooing, and whipping.

The insight here is that 21st-century gay men are the new versions of ancient monks. An insightful book is *Ordinary People as Monks and Mystics: Lifestyles for Self-Discovery,* Marsha Sinetar, Paulist Press, 1986.

OTHER HANDS, OTHER INTENTIONS

Maybe, just maybe—and all the words above may be just a hunk of crap—to surrender completely to other hands and other intentions in total handballing, bondage, whipping, and tit/cock/ball torture is a wholesome, balanced, *yinyang* discipline, necessary in these mad, mad, mad, mad millennial times. Also, as *Desiderata* counsels: "Beyond a wholesome discipline, be gentle with yourself." You decide. How much. How far. How deep. How often. All this is up to you. At your own risk. Listen to no one. However, sent out already as a Gay Man in the Galaxy, can you afford not to risk everything to make your finite self infinite? *Conan the Barbarian* challenged: "Do you want to live forever?" Who doesn't? So live long. Prosper. Auntie Mame shouted, "Life is a banquet and most poor suckers are starving to death!" Blanche DuBois said, "I've always depended on the strangeness of fingers."

Fisting may be a very sophisticated sex-game that could keep your ass and your act together. Guys who haven't tried it shouldn't maybe knock it. Most of fisting's politically correct *critiquenistas* don't need fisting, because they already have their heads stuffed up their butts. Whatever. A man leading an active sex life of external skin-sex often needs the alternative balance of a long, quiet, contemplative sub-skin fisting scene. All he has to do is find an excellent partner to Top him. Relax into his Inner Zygote. Get off on where he goes when he takes the Offramp to Alpha-Centauri, and grow more human, more his own Self, from the experience.

TIME AND ASS ON MY HANDS: FROM STONEHENGE TO NOTRE DAME

Fisting—because the ass-ring may be a circular clock like Stonehenge—has traditionally been used to mark time. All those New Year's Eves at the Slot. The July 4, 1976, Bicentennial Party at the Catacombs where, by Steve McEachern's plan, 50 tops mutualized 50 bottoms simultaneously while—on a monitor set up for the night—the United States Marine Corps Band played live on TV "The Stars and Stripes Forever." To me, the ultimate way to usher in the Ideal New Year's Eve would be getting fisted, while fisting, at the stroke of midnight on the high altar of the Cathedral of Notre Dame in Paris!

So, my darlings, as we all head inexorably to the Exit Ramp of this plane and planet, consider yourself lucky to be a Hand Puppet of the Sex Gods. Remember: You can never be your Self until you're turned completely Inside Out!

Jack Fritscher, says the **Bay Area Reporter**, *"invented the South of Market prose style and its magazines." He is the founding San Francisco editor of* **Drummer,** *and the author of fifteen books including the pioneering* **Leather Blues** *(1968); the first book on leather BDSM rituals* **Popular Witchcraft** *(1972, new edition 2005);* **Some Dance to Remember: A Memoir-Novel of San Francisco 1970-1982** *(new edition 2005); and the erotic-bio of his bicoastal lover,* **Mapplethorpe: Assault with a Deadly Camera.**

His 69 Stories of Leather BDSM Fetish are published in the award-winning 4-volume series: **Corporal in Charge of Taking Care of Captain O'Malley; Stand by Your Man; Rainbow County** *and* **Titanic: 12 Forbidden Stories Hollywood Forgot.** *His coffee-table book of 55 fetish photographs titled* **Jack Fritscher's American Men** *was published in Britain. Since 1982, he has shot nearly 200 videos for his company www.PalmDriveVideo.com. For more information on homomasculine culture visit www.Jack Fritscher.com and www.PalmDriveVideo.com. His leather history analysis is free at www.JackFritscher.com. Books available at Amazon.com.*

First Hand:
An Erotic Guide
To Fisting

E Morse

I want to feel your heart beat
From the inside.
To dance inside you with my fingertips,
To feel you with my glove covered hand,
To make an intimate connection with your soul,
I want to feel your heart beat
From the inside.

>Ed Moore
>Washington DC, 2005

A Boner Book

ONE: YOUR BODY

Everybody has an ass. That established, we can start working our way into it. The anus itself, which most people view as the asshole, is primarily two muscle groups. The external sphincter is the one controlled by your central nervous system. Your own thoughts can "tell" it what to do (i.e. clinch or relax). The muscles of the internal sphincter are controlled by the autonomic nervous system, same as your heart and lungs. To a small extent, it is "trainable." But for the most part it is your external sphincter that, as a bottom, you'll need to acclimate a degree of self-control over.

The rectum is a pretty strong muscular area, and tends to be between six and nine inches long. Like the anus, it has a pretty amazing capacity for expansion, but it is not going to just stretch out like a balloon on the first try. Patience is a must! If you feel a great amount of pain, it's likely that you aren't ready yet. Take the time to experiment with safe objects, like smaller butt plugs and dildos, and use lots of lube. Keep in mind: anything too large for the untrained rectum could lacerate it.

For those who want to get into depth handball, you have to consider the colon. Divided into four parts, it consists of the ascending, transverse, descending and sigmoid colons. The ascending colon leads from the stomach up to the transverse colon. As its name implies, the transverse colon crosses from one side of your body to the other, and connects to the descending colon. The descending colon connects to the sigmoid colon, which, in turn, leads to your rectum. The main function of the colon is to gently shift fecal matter along its many folds towards the rectum, where it is essentially stored until you find a place to release it. After all, we spend much of our early childhood learning to control that storage and release function. One of the other primary purposes of the colon is to absorb water from our wastes so when our body waste arrives at the rectum, it is in a relatively solid form. That's what allows you to use Crisco in liberal amounts, because it's vegetable shortening and your intestine will treat it like it's food.

The sigmoid colon can measure up to 40 cm (about 16 inches) in length, so most of the arm-length fisting prospects will be explored here. It is attached to your pelvic cavity by the sigmoid mesocolon, a series of membranes that gives it great flexibility. Where the sigmoid colon meets the descending colon, there is a slight bend, and the attachment to the pelvic wall is less flexible. If you plan on going for depth fisting, this is very important. Trying to force your hand into an immobile barrier could result in a tear in the colon wall, which is the most serious danger while fisting.

Anatomically, fisting is a comparatively safe activity. Doctors frequently relax a patient's anal muscles for surgery with anesthesia with no ill effects. The key to safety is plenty of patience and common sense. If you're a bottom and you're new to fisting, go slow! If there is unreasonable pain, there is no shame in stopping and trying later, perhaps after a little at home training with dildos. If you're a top and you feel your hand meeting with resistance, don't force it. A little finger wiggling and gentle probing will serve everyone better than trying to bully your way.

You should also remain aware of that which can go wrong in a fisting session. The most common is mucosal laceration, which is a cut in the mucosal lining of your colon or rectum. At worst, it may require stitching; but normally it will heal with antibiotics. You may also tear a muscle from over expanding the anal canal. It's equivalent to tearing a shoulder muscle, and the cure for one of those is to just allow it to heal on its own. Again, patience is the watchword!

The most serious danger is tearing open the bowel. If you break through the muscle wall of the colon, you're on your way to the hospital. Perforation of the bowel leads to peritonitis (contamination of the peritoneum – the lining of the abdominal cavity) and requires surgery. Peritonitis, if left untreated, is frequently fatal. This injury most often takes place at the joint where the sigmoid colon attaches to the descending colon.

Although your asshole has a lot of nerve endings, it is important to understand that your colon doesn't. Your intestine actually suffers hundreds of minor cuts yearly, from roughage like seeds or bones. You just don't feel them. Serious damage to the intestinal wall won't be felt for perhaps hours after the fact. If you feel accumulating pain that increases over time, or cramping, get checked immediately.

Along with the aforementioned common sense and patience, there are plenty of steps you can use to avoid damage to your partner or yourself. Using latex gloves will cover calluses and fingernails, which can scratch. If you must go barehanded, clip your nails beforehand and then use an emery board to file any sharp points down. Use generous amounts of lube. While you're inside your bottom, keep your hand closed in the fist formation. There's less chance of poking or scratching that way. And even if it is overstating the obvious, don't go into a play session if you or the person you're with isn't sober. If your ability to make a value judgment on pain or safety concerns is impaired by drugs or alcohol, you shouldn't be playing inside someone else's guts. Even more so if you're the bottom.

If you think your regular doctor can deal with the information and you are a habitual fister, it certainly doesn't hurt to let him know what your hobby is about. Unless your doctor is gay or kinky, it's highly probable that he won't have the vaguest idea what handballing is. While bearing in mind that physicians can harbor the same kind of prejudice and ignorance about non-vanilla sexual activity as the general population, it will also give him a heads up if you have to pay him a visit should something actually go wrong. Better that he know the possibilities before one falls onto his exam table.

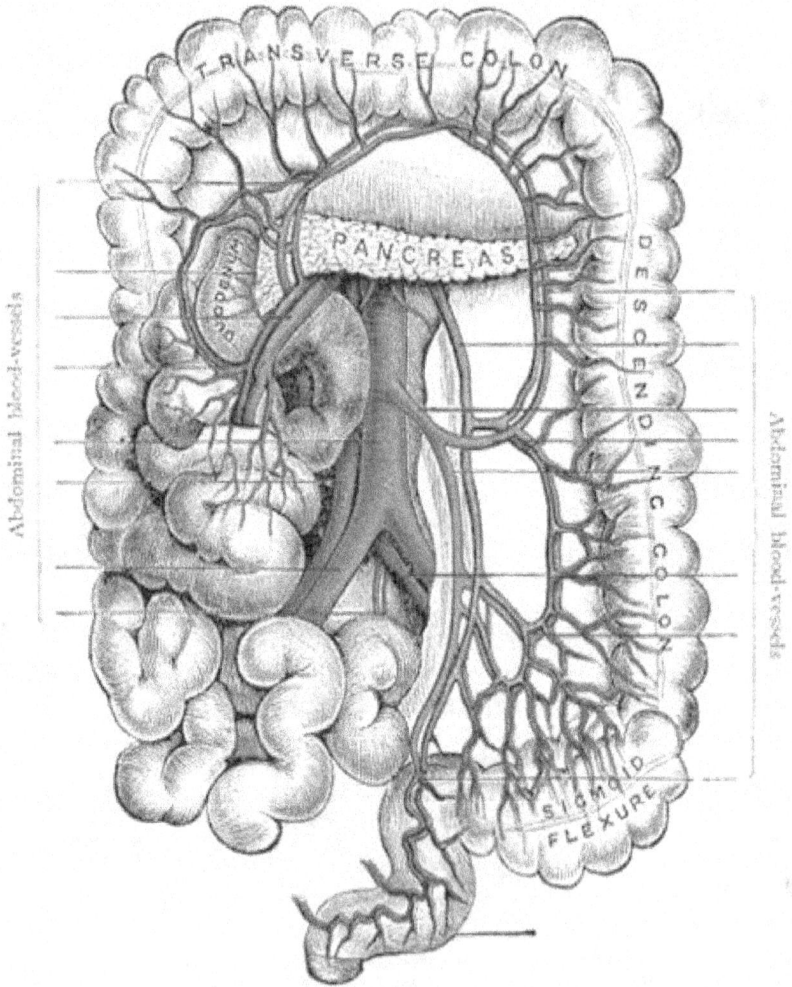

TWO: THE DOCTOR IS REALLY IN

Dr. Peter Johns and his partner DM have been together for seven years. Dr PJ is an HIV and AIDS specialist, and DM is a licensed massage therapist. They requested that their real names not be used in First Hand*, but did sit with me during CLAW in Cleveland, Ohio, April 2005, for this interview. They live in upstate New York.*

Tim Brough: Okay, the first question I ask everybody is what is it primarily that you get out of fisting?

Dr. PJ: Fisting comes partly as a fulfillment of exploring sexual fantasies. Pleasuring someone with a fist, in turn, gives me pleasure.

TB: What, your only fantasies are having—to be fisted?

PJ: Well, all of my fantasies have some anal orientation or component, and always have. So once I came out and discovered the options, it was years from the first time I actually had fantasies about fisting somebody until it physically finally happened.

TB: Was it real?

PJ: No. For me, extreme sex is very intense, and the sensations around the anus are intense. I started out liking men both anally and orally. I also like to look at chests and asses and things like that. One thing leads to another, and you first get into vanilla sex as a young man coming out. Then gradually you've had it with vanilla sex so you're looking for a little variety. While I was doctoring in the Albany area, one of the male nurses invited me to a dungeon party in Saratoga Springs. I had never been out and about in the community, never really been exposed to fist fucking, but getting a lot of other experience with variations of vanilla sex, anal intercourse and more. Basically, it was a dungeon party and that's where I learned about fisting for the first time, and enemas, and all these variations on a theory of, I guess you could say, beyond vanilla sex or extreme sex. I saw people getting fisted, and it intrigued me, so I bought a butt plug. I figured that would be a way to get used to it gradually, to see if I could do it. We had a porn shop across the street from where I lived, so I bought a large butt plug, which really was small compared to some people's fists, and worked on it for two weeks. It wouldn't go in! I was almost ready to take it back, but I don't think they would've, but I finally got it in. And then I thought, whoa, how am I going to get this out! But I got it in and out. If I could get this in and out, I figured a small fist would be the next step. If that could go in, then I'm kind of calm about it.

So then I went to another dungeon party and met this really hot guy. I was just so overwhelmed by his sexual aura, he probably could have done anything to me, but he got his fist in for the first time. I was new to the dungeon scene, new to all this stuff, but I was ready for him to try it. The nurse who originally introduced me to these dungeon parties offered me poppers, and I just didn't want an altered sense. I wanted to do this safely and sanely and have all my senses about me. Other than a Midol, which he said would help me get loosened up, I didn't really take any other drugs and he got in me. I apparently bled a little bit on the sheets and didn't realize it, so I got the Miss Piggy award for that night, 'cause I got opened up for the first time. But he was a hot man, it was a lot of fun, and after that I had it done a couple times more from people. Then I told some of my friends about it. One of my friends said, well yeah, I can try that, so I lubed up his fist and he got it up there and he says, now what? He wasn't really into it, so it was like, okay, it got up there, that was the accomplishment, and that was the end of that. Really, it was only after I met DM that I really got into top fisting and enjoying it, 'cause DM enjoyed so much to get it. We took turns, actually, he fisted me first. Got up there first before his poor ass got finally expanded 'cause he wasn't used to my size fist, I guess.

TB: Your hands only look to be about moderate.

PJ: They're moderate, yes. Now he's become an ass pig. But I could hardly get in him for the first year. Remember?

DM: Well, it'd been a long time since anyone had.

TB: How long ago was that?

PJ: I was in a residency program in the Albany, NY area. A male nurse working in one of he hospitals there invited me to one of these parties before AIDS was even heard of, so these parties were wild. No condoms, no gloves, nothing. In spite of that it was clean, because there were sinks where you could wash, and there were enemas, Clorox and everything, even before AIDS was around. I think it was about 1980, and by 1983 these parties were still going on a little bit. The sanitary things were even more noticeable at this dungeon party and people were more aware. I think it was 1980 that I was first informed of that, '80 or '81, then by '83 we started using the safe sex and the gloves. I moved away from the Albany area in '88, although the dungeon parties had pretty much calmed down by '84 or '85, because of HIV being around and people were getting sick.

TB: The question I give to everyone at this point is, if you can, please describe the most memorable fisting experience you've had. Let's start with DM.

DM: I would be surprised if you didn't get a lot of people telling you about their first one, because it holds a special place in my memory and I've had other friends share the same. For me, my most memorable was the first time, which was in the early to mid 1980's in Frankfurt, Germany. It was a man that I loved and respected on many different levels. He was, for me, a role model of the kind of leather man I wanted to be one day. At the time of the actual event, we'd gotten together and had several play dates before it actually was successful. By the third time we got together, he was with a new partner. We were never really partners or lovers, we were just very good friends, and had great sex. But he ended up getting his fist in me while he had his cock and balls both in his current boyfriend's butt. For me there isn't any way that two men can be more intimate, and it's an interesting exchange of power, because as much as you have to submit to it on a receptive end, at the same time it's very empowering because you're ultimately the one completely in control. The interesting thing was that he was already very ill from AIDS and it really wasn't an issue.

TB: And, of course PJ, that same question for you.

PJ: Well, it's hard to pick out one, although again, your first one is always memorable. Like I mentioned before, this one guy was just a hot man and was willing to introduce me to this, to kind of encourage me through it and the sensations. I'd had a butt plug up my ass, but the sensation of a hot man playing with you, caring about you, expanding your ass beyond its last limit; it was just incredibly sensual and sexy. So I came pretty quickly when that happened! After that it was interesting receiving, but I have also an experience that was pretty hot giving. It was at one of these dungeon parties in the early '80's, and there was the dungeon down in this Saratoga mansion basement. We had several slings and enema tables, and upstairs was where you would rest during these parties. They had movies on and they were watching *The Women* with Joan Crawford, and there's a half-naked guy sitting on the couch watching. I notice coming out of his butt is this leather string. So I said, just out of curiosity, what is that leather string coming out of your butt? And he says, come down to the basement, throw me up in the sling and I'll show you. We went down there; I put him in the sling and he told me to pull it. I pulled on it and pulled on it, and it was a leather thong tied to the middle of a big double-headed dildo, which was folded in half and stuck up there. This big dildo came out, then he puts his leather hat on me and he's going, woof, woof, now you're my Master, shove your fist up there! He was so turned on, that I got my fist lubed up and put it in. It was a real turn-on making him feel good, he was just writhing in pleasure from my fist going up there, and he wanted it more and more. I got up to the elbow, and as a doctor, I'm thinking, oh my God, is this safe? What's going on? I could feel his prostate, then I got up past the sigmoid colon, and I got up to my elbow and could feel his spleen. What a way to palpate a spleen! I knew I was up at what's called the splenic flexure

11

and couldn't go past that, but he was just in seventh heaven and I was enjoying it, but also as a doctor thinking, well, there's the aorta, there's the spleen, from an internal exam, it was amazing. It was quite an experience.

TB: One of the things I should ask you, as a doctor, as far as the elements of danger involved for fisting from an HIV and health aspect, I'm assuming that gloves do keep you fairly safe.

PJ: Yes, they do. If you have little micro-tears in your nails or your hands or whatever, the mucous of the anus is fairly rich in HIV virus, if you're positive and not on medicine that suppresses it. If you get that mucous in contact with little open cuts or sores on a hand or a forearm, you can conceivably pick up HIV that way, but the glove will protect the main parts of your hand, which is where the surface area is. Most forearms are not going to be cut or anything. If they are, you want a long glove. Most people are careful with their hygiene when they're fisting. And even if you don't have open sores or any problems with your hands, generally the skin is a wonderful barrier against HIV. Again, you want to be careful and wash before getting onto other things, but the mucous of the rectum is rich in HIV-related cells and virus particles, if you're not suppressed on your medicine. So there is a chance of picking it up or transferring it to somebody else if you're not careful.

TB: Now, HIV from a top's aspect, if you're HIV positive as a top.

PJ: If you have intact skin you're not going to give it to your bottom, glove or not

TB: But the glove's still the most effective barrier?

PJ: They are an effective barrier, but when you get deeper and if you're talking about the normal glove, you're going to go past your glove. As long as you're careful with that, if you're the top and you don't have open sores or cuts, it's really not a problem to transmit or receive.

TB: When cleaning out, an enema is also taking away the microbes.

PJ: Right. What can happen with an enema and douching is fresh water flowing. As a doctor, I don't always know how to answer my patients, but people who douche a lot can leach out potassium and electrolytes. I have not had problems personally or with most people, but occasionally with the electrolyte changes, during the scene your muscles could cramp more easily. It strips the mucosal lining, the protective mucous out of the colon, and a lot of the stool. With that clean of a colon, it takes away some of the natural bacterial flora. It is possible, and I've seen this happen with people who fist and clean, to get what is called clostridium difficile, which causes a diarrhea. You need to treat that with an antibiotic in order for the diarrhea to settle down. But in general, fresh water douching is all right for the colon.

Orange juice is probably the easiest thing to use to replace potassium, probably as much as bananas; yogurt will replace the washed-out bacterium.

DM: Acidophilus cultures - you can get it at health food stores like GNC. Because a great many yogurts are pasteurized, they vary in qualities of the live acidophilus and bifidopholus cultures that are in them. Therefore, you could eat a crappy yogurt and still not replace the flora in your gut. For people who have dairy issues, yogurt's not really an option, so powders are a way to get the cultures back in you.

The bigger issue with douching isn't as much the depletion of the cultures as much as the depletion of the mucosal lining. Often, when we're douching, we're in a hurry because we're hot, bothered and there's somebody waiting; you really want to get to whatever you want to be doing.

PJ: Really, to do a good cleaning takes at least an hour. Don't ever think you can shortcut it. You may think you're done, then you're in the scene and more stuff's coming down!

DM: There is a classic standard abdominal massage protocol for helping people with constipation. When we were at the Delta Run, I shared it with the men at the fisting forum. It is good for cleaning out, prepping and getting ready for a session. It does two things. It helps get the water and the waste out of the bowel, and at the same time, it is relaxing any spasm you've created by the trauma of the douching. When you get all this water up there, it causes your smooth muscle to go into spasm. At which point, your sphincters lock down and you can't get the water out. This massage technique is used for people who have constipation, and it's really great for helping to clean out the large intestinal tract. At the same time, it stimulates peristaltic movement, the natural movement for the muscles in that area. Any spasm that wants to happen, you're helping to alleviate it.

PJ: It's got a cute name, too. It's called the "I love you" massage.

DM: The person starts by lying on his left side, so you have gravity assisting you in the way you want the stuff to flow. After you've douched and you think you're cleaned out, you lay down on your left side. Starting up under where your spleen is, you apply pressure, and gently, with constant pressure, stroke down the descending colon. You do that several times, in a straight line. That's the "I".

After you do that several times, you go over to the beginning of the transverse colon, and you stroke across it to the left. You have to relax each section of the tract before you tie them together. So you've relaxed the descending colon first, you relax the transverse colon, and then you tie them together. When you do that, you're creating the "L" for love. You go across the top of the abdomen and down, across and down.

You then go to the beginning, where your appendix is, and you start with the ascending colon. You massage and relax the ascending colon. After you have massaged that area several times, you tie all three together. That first movement is the "I" the second movement is the 'L' and the final is the "U." When they're teaching massage students to do this, they call it the "I Love You." It's a little self-love that you do between the cleaning out session and before you jump in the sling. It also helps with trapped gas.

After we had the session at Delta, there was a big play party that night in the fisting cabin. I saw a bunch of the attendees at the dinner the next day and they were telling me "thanks, that works great!"

Some guys will completely change their diet for three days before they know they're having a heavy fisting weekend. Other guys won't, and there are other alternatives, like Immodium or Midol. After you've been doing it for years, you'll know your own system. You also know, based on the quality of what's coming out, whether you're getting waste from the descending colon or the transverse colon. What happens is that people clean out the descending colon, and think they're good to go. At the same time, you're stimulating peristaltic movement of the large intestine. What that's going to do is push all the stuff from the transverse colon over to the descending colon. So by starting two hours before, you're giving time to at least clean out the second third of the entire large intestinal tract. Usually, unless you're going for an all-nighter, this should suffice for you. It's also a totally different story with guys that are going up to the shoulder! In San Francisco, when it's Folsom Street Fair time, there's a line around the block at the colonic clinic. Everybody's getting a high colonic before the weekend.

TB: Just for the good old basic stuff involved with fisting, please describe the dangers involved when you've got your hand in there.

PJ: Sometimes, you could technically perforate a colon. You hear what are called urban legends, famous stories about the light bulb that was stuck up there, which may happen. But I think if it happens once, you'll hear about it a thousand times, as if this happens all the time.

TB: And then with a different person.

NR: Right, exactly. I have not personally heard of anybody getting a perforated colon from that kind of thing. You can get cramps, but I personally am not aware of that. Of course, there's bleeding if you have hemorrhoids or warts, then you can irritate anal fissures and similar things. But actually a lot of people who are fisted, by having the anus stretched and worked at, don't have problems with hemorrhoids or fissures because the anus is getting so much attention. The other thing you hear about is, if you're fisted a lot, that you'll become incontinent and lose your stool. It can happen that, after you've been loosened up, your muscles there aren't quite tight enough to hold things in as they could be and there is leakage once in a while. But there's not total incontinence where you have to wear diapers all the time. Though I can think of a couple of my patients that are into fisting that are permanently loose, they don't loose their stool. That's a very rare complication as well.

The other complication you hear about is called rectal prolapse, where you have a loose rectal sphincter and then part of the rectum actually comes out and is visible. Although you can see that on purpose on people who have been fisted a lot, they'll be able to suck that right back up and the sphincter will hold it in. So rectal prolapse is unusual from people who get fisted a lot as well, unless there's a pathological underlying cause for rectal prolapse.

TB: Is that what's commonly referred to as the rosebud?

NR. The rosebud, yes, even a huge rosebud would be kind of like a rectal prolapse. Unless there's some other underlying medical condition, having a real problem with a rectal prolapse would be highly unusual.

DM: There are sites like asspig.com. It's a really interesting place to form a network with men that are into fisting. It's fascinating for me; just last week I was reading that there was this guy who has, as his ultimate goal, to get his anus to double prolapse. He wants to get stretched to the point that he has the world's biggest rosebud. Is it a medical malady if you want it?

The thing is, PJ's a Doctor, and I'm a massage therapist. I spend all day getting people's bodies to trigger their own healing responses and to create tone and efficiency for the human body. What is fisting if not really intense rectal massage? This whole thing about not being able to hold your stool; it is actually quite the opposite! Think about it. By massaging the area, you're bringing more tone and vitality to the area. I can make guys cry by clamping down. I can break your arm if I don't let go!

PJ: (Laughing) That's true.

DM: It has totally to do with the person's approach to it. I've been active in the fisting environment for twenty years and I could still probably break somebody's forearm with my sphincter.

TB: I've had several people tell me "My asshole is trained."

DM: That's true! As much as you have to train it and learn to control relaxing the sphincter in order to allow somebody in, the exact opposite can come into play, too. I have a stronger, healthier asshole now. An interesting thing is, in 1991, I had to have the first three inches of my rectum cauterized all the way around because of anal warts. Talk about something painful! Try having your first bowel movement after having that treatment done! I tore the walls down in my bathroom! Yet even after something as radical as that happening, the most intense assplay I've gotten into has been after that fact, not before.

TB: What do you do to get men that are being fisted to relax and expand?

PJ: The more uptight you are about that happening, especially if it's a first time, the more your muscles will go into spasms. You can use poppers, they do relax your smooth muscles a little bit. Some people are not ready to go beyond just a fist in their anal cavity. There are valves in there, called the sigmoid colon valves. They're like kinks you have to get up and above. When you get up to the sacroiliac area, there's a bone you have to get over and you can feel that. We call it 'the shelf.' You get into the pelvic area, and there's a cup-like area that holds your hand. To get beyond that and the colon, you have to go on top of 'the shelf,' which is, basically, up along your lumbar spine. To get through all those folds, for some people, they're just too sensitive and you'll never do it. Other people train their ass and train their colon to relax and get them a little farther up.

TB: I've gotten that from several people, about deep fisting. I've a hard time fathoming getting past your elbow, and they want it all they way up to the shoulder. Although I've spoken with men that have!

PJ: You're going to hit the diaphragm up there by the spleen.

DM: Until you learn how to make that turn from the descending colon to the transverse colon, you can seriously hurt somebody.

PJ: Unless you are really experienced with this, unless the bottom is really experienced with this, then neither of you should be doing this.

DM: Yes, exactly. There must be a very open communication. We're just in the physical aspects here, but there's a physical, emotional, mental and spiritual component to any human interaction. When you get into extreme human interaction, like fisting…

PJ: Which is a real increased level of trust, intimacy, more than vanilla sex.

DM: So your question was, what do you do to get somebody to relax? It all depends on the individual. Are there physical things you can do? Yes, if you understand the anatomy of where you're going and what you're doing. There are certain manipulations you can do. But everyone is different, so you have to do what feels best for the person receiving. I've had some tops that are very experienced with their partner. They have an extensive fisting history with one person, but it becomes different with another! So they're looking to expand their understanding. Sometimes it's physical, sometimes it's mental, sometimes emotional, and sometimes spiritual. For one person to say that one aspect of it is bullshit is their perspective on the situation.

If you want to talk about the emotional or spiritual aspects of taking a fist and taking a fist deep, you're talking about the first three chakras. They're all based in the in the physical. As a massage therapist in New York State, I have an extensive training in traditional Chinese medicine, the human energy systems and the chakras. It can be a component of it without you even being conscious of it. If you're willing to embrace it, just like you're willing to embrace the concept of taking somebody's fist up your ass, then you might be opening the door for a greater level of depth to the experience. To open yourself up to your place of personal power is pretty intense. There are multiple dimensions to the experience, and people come to the experience from their own place of understanding, and seek the place of understanding from the person they're doing the act with. Other people may be looking for a more expansive understanding, and will delve into it in different directions.

It's very interesting, I think, that in the SM community, that fisting can be part of an SM act, but someone who is exclusively into fisting isn't considered necessarily SM. When you go to things like the Delta Run, it's separated out. Sometimes for practical reasons, like logistics and cleanliness.

TB: I also think it's because that, for any fetish, there's a certain category of things that, for you, become number one on the priority list. For me, it's bondage; if I'm not tied up, it isn't any fun. For a lot of folks, fisting is the dominant act for their kink psyche. I'd say right after trust and intimacy, control is the big thing that people have mentioned they get from fisting. They like the fact that they can control another person's body via the act of putting their arm in it. The fact that everything is now, no pun intended, riding on their hand. Or the aspect of being able to reach in there far enough that you can feel that person's pulse. That is a strong control, dominance and submission issue, so for a lot of people there is that 'I'm going to take you where you've never been' type thing. But also for a lot of people, there are ones who've told me that they would not allow anyone to fist them if they'd come up and say "I'm Top only."

PJ: Yes! A lot of times you have to be that way! My first experiences were as a bottom, and I can still bottom. Sometimes you get into a top mode and that's kind of fun, but I'd rather have somebody who has experienced both!

I wasn't trained, you know. As a doctor, I'd delivered lots of babies before I'd put my fist in somebody. When I did get around to fisting, I thought *this is like the female pelvis.* I could figure out the landmarks. When babies come out, they always come out of the vagina sideways. Then, as they come out, the head will spin and there's almost a screwing motion. Now, when you put your fist into an ass, you start in a certain way, and as you turn your fist, it will go through. Just like a baby coming out! So I discovered, just through that experience, an easier way to get inside people.

DM: It also depends on how you define the term 'trained.' My friend Jim, who was the first person to ever fist me, was personally a mentor to me. I question if he ever had a perception that he was ever that to or for me. We have another friend, who, anytime he has the opportunity to get his hand up my butt, he's there. He's 95% Top, and he's happiest with his fist up somebody else, not with somebody's fist up his. It goes back to what I'd said earlier about people with limited experience. He's been with his partner for years and years, to the elbow and very intense, but it's sort of always the same. It is interesting, because he comes to me and asks questions, and we have sex, and even though I'm the one in the receptive position, I'm kind of mentoring for him. It's an interesting dynamic and very fluid.

TB: Along with poppers, what do people use for relaxing into the scene?

PJ: Poppers do loosen up smooth muscle, which is a lot of what your rectum is composed of. You have voluntary muscle and smooth muscle, which are the involuntary. By relaxing smooth muscle, they relax the sphincter, and relax the blood vessels, which is why you get that rush. You get your blood pressure lowering, some people associate that with the pleasure. Unfortunately, for loosening up, some people do use street drugs.

Some people also use things meant for menstrual cramping. Menstrual or uterine cramping is smooth muscle spasm. So when you're getting fisted, your smooth muscle can go into spasm in your colon. Anything that is used for menstrual cramping will help colon cramping as well.

DM: I've spoken to many fisting bottoms who won't get into a sling until they've smoked a joint.

PJ: Can I tell a funny story? As a doctor, I know DM cleans himself out well. But I thought I felt a little ball of poop left up there. Then I noticed it was always in the same spot after a couple of times. I thought then that it must be a colon polyp, about 22 cm in. I said to him that you need a colonoscopy because you have a polyp. I called up my G.I. specialist and told him, "my patient has a colon polyp at 22 cm, and it's about 1 ½ cm big" because I could feel it. He gets the colonoscopy and sure enough that's what it was…

DM: At 22 cm in!

PJ: Exactly. It was funny because the GI Specialist never asked how I knew that, because I don't do colonoscopies or sigmoidoscopies, but I was able to describe it, size it and tell him where it was to find it. He removed it and DM hasn't had any problems since. I checked, so there's good medical follow-up, too!

DM: I go to the colonoscopy clinic, and I have medical issues with anesthesia. It makes me deathly ill. Being that I really like anyone playing with my ass anyway, I figure I'm doing this without drugs. So I get on the gurney and decline all the medications, which they all thought was a little disturbing. The three nurses come, and of course they all wound up being women, and I'm on the gurney with my gown on. They wheel me through the general corral, where you've got everyone behind curtains doing the same thing. They turn the corner into the exam room, and they run my gurney right into the doorframe. I say, "God, you're a bad driver. Please tell me you're not the one that's running the scope."

And she goes, "Oh yeah, I am the one that's running the scope!" I come to find out, not only is she running the scope, she's a trainee and it's her first day. I was begging them to let her do one of the people who are drugged! But they got in there and they did find the polyp, and it was exactly where PJ said. I got some pretty pictures of it. I wanted to make it into a Christmas card, but we decided it wasn't exactly the best idea.

THREE: PLAYING

The Toy Bag

Just about anyone who plays, be it handball or any other esoteric sexual activity, usually carries a toy bag. Just what should the well-prepared fist aficionado carry on his person? Since fisting isn't really toy intensive, you can keep it to basics.

GLOVES: Since the onset of the AIDS era, gloves have become widely available. Latex gloves can be found in almost any drug, hardware and even grocery store. Try to find ones that aren't powdered, as the powder can sometimes irritate the ass they are about to enter. Don't be stingy. Buy yourself plenty. Make sure you get the right size; too small and they might tear during play, too large and they can bunch up and make the play difficult. Once you're done playing with your gloves, dispose of them. Also bear in mind that, like condoms, the latex for gloves will deteriorate if exposed to petroleum products or too much sunlight.

LUBRICANTS: Throughout the interviews conducted for this book, one thing became obvious. Crisco remains the all-around all-time favorite for fisting. When picking up your supply for the evening, be sure you get the can without additives. A can of vegetable shortening remains sterile until it is open, so make sure that when you go out, you have a fresh stock in the bag. Never use your can for more than one person's butt. If you're headed for a party, don't hesitate to make it a BYOC event. At some parties, bowls are set out so scoops from cans can be portioned out to individual stations. Be generous! Remember that sliding a hand in and out of an ass produces friction, and lubing your gloves up will keep the bottom from unnecessary heat and discomfort. And if you're choosing vegetable shortening from the grocer's, Bill Freyer of the Red Hankies Of San Diego offered this piece of advice. "If you use a generic store brand shortening, it won't have the individual additives or the added smell. It won't get that rancid after-smell like Crisco does."

Popular commercial brands such as Elbow Grease and Lube are okay, as long as they are vegetable based. The advantage here is that they tend to not have that "Mineshaft" odor of Crisco, and won't go rancid as quickly. Petroleum based lubes are not recommended, as they can damage the mucosal lining of the rectum. Water-based lubes, like Wet and KY, tend to dry out during play relatively quickly, and you'll get the kinky equivalent of rug-burn. Any kind of lotion that contains perfumes or additives can be irritants, and should be left on the store counter.

If you are going to use the individual bowls for your handball station, make sure to wash them thoroughly once the play period has ended. Or just throw them away.

MANICURE: Keep a set of fingernail clippers handy, as well as an emery board. If you're going to put your digits up someone's ass, clip the nails to the quick. Use the emery board to make sure that any sharp points have been filed away. When filing the nails down, remember to file the edges from the top of the nail and down, across the tip of your finger. That lessens the chance for a sharp edge to remain pointing up from the fingertips.

DOUCHE: There are plenty of devices on the market to get the shit out of your system. While just about every top interviewed here suggested strongly that a visiting bottom should be well cleaned out before play begins, a small bulb douche that you can take along is always handy. You can get them from reputable fetish gear companies or in your local drug store. Avoid the brands that include chemical additives and stick to the plain water cleanout. For the home model, you can get a shower nozzle attachment at just about any housewares store. These shower bidets go by many brand names, like *Shower Shot*, *Silver Bullet*, etc., and are easy to install. There's always the omnipresent red bag with attached nozzle, which you hang high enough to allow gravity to flow the water in. The advantage to the red bags is mostly scenic, but they are usually made of a heavy-duty rubber that is durable and resists wear and tear nicely. One traveling fister commented that he packs a turkey baster in is luggage, as it is less likely to exact a "what is this" question from luggage inspectors. The key to using any of these items is your personal comfort level.

PAPER TOWELS: Fisting is a greasy activity. Expect a mess. If you are in the middle of a really heavy session and you're really laying on the Crisco, you can plan on the need to wipe off the excess. Having that roll of towels by the sling is always a handy thing. (And a readily available waste can isn't a bad idea, either.)

MUSIC: There's nothing like a little music to set the mood. If you have a personal favorite, pack the CD or the tape. If you really want to set the scene to your liking, burn a collection that flows with your expectations of pleasure. The work of Enigma, the chanting of monks, New Age, light jazz, disco or classical; whatever turns you on. The kinky artist known as ButtBoy has created a series of CD's that make great background for playdates. One interviewee told me of how one of his most magical experiences was set to the song *Telegraph Road* by Dire Straits. Just keep in mind that you're trying to set a relaxing mood here. Although I know of men who swear by it, throwing that Heavy Metal Mix anthology in the CD player during the party may get you clubbed.

Cleaning up, cleaning out.

"There was somebody at the bar the one night, he was trying very hard to get picked up by two or three of us. He appeared to be a serious player, but everyone was kind of giving off a very negative vibe towards him. Later the comment happened to be made along the lines of 'I tried to teach him how to clean out, but he still kept showing up without understanding why. He's not worth your time.' Ultimately he didn't leave with anybody."
Anonymous interview

You've got a play date coming up and you really want to be prepared. As the saying goes, cleanliness is next to godliness. As a bottom, you really want to present yourself in the best possible light, and that means getting yourself as thoroughly cleaned out as possible. If you've got a few days' notice, there are a few tips to get some advance preparations before the big night.

You can start by watching what you eat a few days before you plan to play. Eat more foods containing dietary fiber, or add a dose of Metamucil or something similar into your food intake each day. The last 18-24 hours before you play, try to stay away from things like dairy products that will bind you up. Get plenty of fruits and vegetables, while avoiding starchy vegetables (like potatoes and beans) that would give you gas. The day of your play, try to stick to light foods. Pass on the red meats and dairy, as these will bind you. From the time you put something in your mouth to the large intestine usually takes 12 hours, and then add about 12 more before you eliminate it. Logic would then dictate that you should ease up on heavy eating better than 18 hours before meeting your man for the evening. Take a dose of vitamins the morning before you go out, and orange juice or a banana with breakfast will keep your potassium up.

You really should plan on two hours for your clean out. After all, showing up at a Top's place (or vice versa) and having him sitting around waiting while you use the facilities not only will make you rush through what should be a relaxed and thorough activity, it's just bad form. So allow yourself the time to give yourself a proper douching.

Make sure that you use only clean, warm water. If you're using the shower bidet, you really need to be aware of temperature and water pressure. Get yourself into a relaxed position, be it lying down in the tub/shower, standing or squatting. Get the flow of the water to a moderate flow and insert the nozzle tip. Fill yourself up to the point that you feel ready and hold it in as best you can. After a few seconds, let it out. You'll likely have to repeat this process a few times. If you're using the red bag, you may want to keep some water in a bottle or pitcher ready to refill the bag before you go for the second or third round. The bulb douches offer a nice way to relax when cleaning out. If you're in a tub of lukewarm water, you can submerge the bulb and let it fill with water before you insert it, which keeps you from squeezing air into your ass. The drawback is that, once you feel you've sufficiently filled yourself with water, you will probably want to step from the tub to the toilet to relieve yourself. The goal is when you release the water, it's coming out clean. No one can tell you exactly how your body will behave when you're giving yourself an enema, so the main guideline is to practice until you know your own insides.

Make sure to "burp" your bulb or enema hose before you stick it in. If you start squeezing bubbles into your gut, you could cause yourself cramps. If air gets in while you're standing, it rises to the top of the water. (Thus blocking the water from cleaning out what rests above the air pocket.) It's why lying back or lying down while douching can be preferable, as is going at a slower pace. If you think you're stuck, and can't get rid of the air bubble, you can try lying down for a half-hour or so in various positions to help move the water. You can also press gently on your belly, and bounce around a little to see if you can jiggle it loose. (Also see the "I Love You" massage technique in Chapter Two.)

When you're douching yourself out, water is best. Since your large intestine is designed to absorb nutrients and water from the processed food as it moves through, you can expect to urinate during the process. Any kind of additive in your water may become an irritant. Even soaps may have chemical additives that – at worst – will give you a case of nausea. Adding anything to the water you use to clean out will cause the colon to try to absorb it. Even water softeners can make you feel a little off, as they are primarily salts. Unless you're experienced and have experimented with exactly what works for you, use only water. There were those in the interview process who told of using a little baking soda or wine while preparing, but caution is the watchword when thinking of anything else other than basic H2O.

Also bear in mind that the nozzle on your enema device is still a hard, solid, blunt object. Insert it only as far as necessary, and don't use it like it's a butt plug. Once you're done emptying out, clean up! After all, you've just poked the nozzle into your feces, and feces carry germs. Bleach works fine, as does anti-bacterial soap. You should keep your nozzles as clean as your dildos, and really shouldn't share the nozzles.

Meanwhile, as the bottom is at home getting his hygiene in order, what about the man preparing the play space? While fisting isn't exactly an instrument intensive activity, there are still plenty of things you can do to insure that your fisting space is comfortable and prepared. Straighten-up before the guest of honor arrives. If you use your sling as a catch all for loose objects, get them in their proper place. Crack open a fresh can of lube beforehand and let it sit out, lid on, warming to room temperature. Have the paper towels at the ready, as well as plenty of gloves. Put some drinks in the fridge, and maybe stock some after-play snacks. Get candles ready if you like that kind of lighting. Spread some throw rugs or newspaper under the sling if you don't want to have droppings all over the floor.

If a sling isn't part of your play area, then you should have play rugs and sheets set aside specifically for nights like this. If you don't mind having one, get a rubber mattress cover to spread on the bed and cover it with a bed sheet specifically intended for fisting dates. Moving pads and drop cloths are also great for this purpose. If you have any furnishings that you don't want to get grease stained, cover them up or move them out of the room. Put the musical selection in the player so you don't have to finagle a CD or tape with lube-covered fingers. Get plenty of spare towels and disinfectant for cleanup after the play is done. Planning on using toys? Get them in an available location. If your toys extend past the range of dildos and butt stuff, get them where they need to be. There's nothing more embarrassing then trying to fasten up a set of restraints but not being able to find your snap hooks.

Pitching

You've gone through all the preparation and your guest is in the sling, or wherever else you may want him to rest. The music is playing, the lights are dimmed and the candles are flickering. You want this to be a night that both of you can remember.

More than anything, you have to both be in the proper mood. Your bottom may be a little nervous. To relax him, maybe you could stroke his nipples and give them a little pinch to get his excitement level up. A little foreplay will always lighten the tension that may exist and get the energy flowing. Kissing, licking, or a little light body rubbing can make your bottom all the more receptive to that first touch.

You should probably try getting a little lube on the fingertips of your glove and just gently massage his asshole. It will comfort the muscles into relaxing, making that first entry a bit easier. Keep in mind that you don't have to race into this. Give the bottom a taste of your intent, one finger, then maybe two or more. Allow his ass to draw you in, instead of forcing your way. Remember, you're asking that his ass start shifting into reverse. While an experienced player may already have his ass "trained," a less experienced man may not.

As much as people talk about "reading" your bottom, fisting is probably one of the activities where this technique is essential. Follow how his body reacts to your touch. Listen to how he verbalizes. Tune in, as he is probably doing the same with you.

Once you think he's relaxed and ready to accept more, keep your hand in the conical, "swan head" position as you work it in. Use plenty of lube; don't skimp! As previously stated, make sure you have plenty on hand before the evening's festivities begin. You're engaging in an activity that creates friction, and you don't want to find yourself in the middle of an intense experience only to discover your hand has dried out. Allow your fingers to wiggle or stroke the bottom's hole as you press inward, gently. Tease a little. Use pressure, being firm but unhurried.

Pay attention to your bottom's reactions. How is he responding? Is he tensing up? How is his breathing? There's no shame in asking him how it's going. You're giving pleasure here, after all. As you get your fingers deeper in, you may have to stop on occasion to allow him to acclimate. Gently rocking your hands in and out may do the trick. Gracefulness is also a good watchword. Jerking, sudden moves are distracting and will break the flow of your activity and possibly cause your bottom undesired pain.

Once you have eased your "beak" into his ass, you may want to open your fingers a bit. The initial entrance of your full hand into his rectum is a very intense moment. Watch for his reaction, and maybe give him a breather to react and relax again. This is when you can reconfigure your hand into the closed fist, and maybe gently twist it a bit, depending on his reactions, desires and experience. Twisting also helps spread the lube around your arm and his ass! If not, maintain the "swan head" position and explore, gently. Never forget that you are in a fragile area. If you feel resistance, be careful. If it feels bony, stop. There's no need to force blindly ahead. Just allow your fingers and hand to follow the natural curvature of your partner's anus.

This may also be a moment to recollect yourself. Do you need to pull out and re-grease? Ask your bottom if he can handle that. Never jerk away suddenly! Just ease yourself away and coat yourself up if you have to. Maybe your bottom likes having you come all the way out and go back in a second time. Either way, proceed as you feel fit here.

So now you're inside the rectum, bearing in mind that it has the capacity to expand. Gentle rocking and probing will allow that to happen. Get a feel for the structure of where you are, as there are likely some twists in your bottom's anatomy. No two asses are the same. As you get used to playing with a consistent partner, you may become accustomed to his preferences. But it's likely you'll never get the same reaction twice. Take your cues from his reactions, and allow your hand to follow. He'll let you know what's working.

Allow yourself to feed into your shared experience. If you started this session based on a mutual fantasy, permit yourself to drift into it. Maybe you could verbalize the images to him while you're playing inside of his ass. Use your non-fisting hand to stimulate yourself or to play with your partner. Utilize these images to build up the sexual energy between you. Let your own pleasure build along with his, and you can prolong the magic.

Be it orgasm, exhaustion or maybe you've hit your limits; eventually you'll have to draw the session to its close. Once you both feel that you've gone as far as you've wanted for the night, ease out. Again, don't pull out suddenly! Think of the energy and experience you've just shared and allow that to guide your exit. The bottom may even want you to rock your hand in his rectum once more for good measure. Be prepared to ease him down from your lovemaking after you've removed yourself. A little cuddling and moral support can go a long way in making what just transpired truly memorable.

It's also likely that both of you will be thirsty and hungry after you've played. Having some cool water or soda handy is a good idea, and maybe some decent snack foods, fruits etc.

While it is likely that most fist bottoms will be happy to stop at the rectum, there will be those who want it deeper or wider. If you feel you're ready, go for it. But having the equipment handy is a good thing. If your bottom wants to go for depth, it helps to remember the basics of his anatomy. The sigmoid colon is attached to the rectum, and both of these organs are relatively free and mobile from their connections to the pelvic cavity. It's where the sigmoid colon meets the descending colon that the attachment is more rigid.

If your bottom wants you to "go deep," you'll need to use your fingertips to gently search for the first loop of the sigmoid colon. Use your fingers to massage the area open before reaching the entry stage. You'll have to feel around quite a bit before you recognize where you're going. You may have to massage and reach a little before the colon opens up to accept your hand, as the sigmoid colon does a fair amount of looping and twisting. If your bottom registers discomfort or you really feel resistance, stop!

Each twist in the sigmoid colon will require some massage and prompting before it accepts your hand, so go easy. When you feel a more rigid space as you move along, it is probably the curve where the descending colon begins. (The sigmoid colon is usually about six inches in length.) If your bottom is experienced enough to be going this far, then you just need to be extra aware that this is a less flexible area than where your hand has just been. Use your fingertips again, and explore the direction your hand should go. And farther up the line is the transverse colon, which swings from left to right across the gut. That means the bend in the colon is sharp and very tricky to negotiate. Feel your way through it. Don't try to jam it along, but allow the colon to "come to you."

If you're going to go this far, then it is equally important to remember that, as cautious as you were going up, be equally so when coming down. Come out slow, and gauge your bottom's reactions. If he wants you to go deeper, he will likely tell you so, and if you're moving out too quickly, he'll probably tell you that, too. More than anything, you're sharing a ride together. He may just be the passenger on your arm, but he's also your best guide to his inner roadmap.

If your bottom craves width over depth, you're going to have both your hands full. The bottoms that really dig this usually have plenty of practice not only with fists, but also with butt plugs and dildos, and perhaps with the inflatable expanding kind. If you already know your bottom has this preference, be ready ahead of time. Get extra lube and have both gloves on before you start. If your hand goes in with all the difficulty of your pinkie, that is a good indication that he may want something a little more substantial. Of course, he'll probably let you know prior to the commencement of your session. Just remember that, even though this bottom has a very experienced ass, his colon and rectum are just as sensitive as anyone else's and just as prone to injury. If you're about to enter a two-fist man, go just as patiently as you would with anybody else. If anything, be even more cautious because you've replaced a reed with a tree trunk and the physical mass of your own two hands inside of another man can be far more unwieldy than a single fist. Vary your speed, twist around a little more, and use as much lube as you can slather on.

You still need to start with a single hand. For some, the second hand massages around the wrist of the already placed hand, sliding and expanding one finger at time. You can then slide the second hand along the narrow wrist of the first, gradually expanding your bottom's entryway. Or you can fist the bottom with both hands, one at a time, to get him used to the form of your right and left hands. (As each hand is a mirror opposite, this will allow the bottom to acclimate to the structure of each.) Then, when you begin to slide each hand alongside the other past his sphincter, the muscles have already gotten used to the form of both. But you should never just clench your hands together and try to force them in at the same time. Like all other aspects of topping, patience and gradual progress will serve you the best.

For those bottoms that just can't stop, you may find yourself involved with sessions for the true pig. Some will want you clean up past the elbow. This is a challenge for any top, since you're going to have to get past a bony joint. You'll need lots of lube, again. Also be aware that you're going to have to be cautious about bending your arm, should you go that distance. If your bottom is this experienced and hungry, you'll probably view this as a treat. If you aren't prepared to push that far, say no. Admitting to inexperience is a lot easier than explaining to the staff at the local ER.

Although I have not mentioned this much before now, setting the parameters of your session is of paramount importance. There are a lot of things you should know before your bottom arrives. Everything from his experience level to expectations for the evening should be discussed beforehand. Get contact information if necessary. Make sure to ask if he has any medical problems, including very basic questions as to allergies pertaining to latex. There are plenty of alternatives to latex gloves available.

Here is how one of the interviewees responded to the challenge of latex allergies:

"I went to Home Depot and got plastic painter's gloves, since one of my fisting partners has a latex allergy. He prefers bareback to latex, and I don't like bareback, or bare hands, because of damaged cuticles and dirt under the nails. That is why I went to HD and bought the painters' gloves. Since then, I noticed the cast on the one of the network morning shows using food handler's gloves, so now I keep those on hand as an option to latex, and try to get those without a powdered coating."

There will also be those rare bottoms that want your foot up their butts. What can I say other than *EXPERIENCED ONLY!* The bones of the foot just aren't as fluid as the ones in your hand, and the nerves in your hand are much more sensitive than those in your foot. The shape of the foot is also far more rigid. I didn't get too many interviewees that spoke of footing, but Bill Gardner of Hot Desert Knights (as one who has actually witnessed the event) put it thusly; "You need a really sloppy asshole and a very tiny foot."

I did manage to find one individual who was willing to give me his story about the night the foot became the object of attention. We'll visit his story in the following chapter.

CATCHING:

As a bottom, you really have to do a fair amount of mental preparation, along with the physical cleaning out. If you're a beginner, you may have to understand that you aren't going to take a hand the size of a ham-hock on round one. The circumference of most hands ranges between ten to fifteen inches, and the smaller the hand, the easier it will be for you to take. If you are a novice, make sure to tell your top! If he is experienced, he's just as likely to share your concerns about how the session goes and that your desire is to come away with a positive experience. Bear in mind that, like learning concert piano, you're not going to Carnegie Hall on the first date.

To that extent, you may want to give yourself a few early training sessions, be it with buttplugs and dildos, or just a little self-help with your own fingers.

Get yourself washed, lube yourself thoroughly and explore. By learning to accommodate an item in your ass, you'll become more relaxed when it comes time to take your first hand from someone else. These training sessions will also become useful in that you're training your ass muscles to react to touch, pressure and other stimuli. Once you learn what makes you react positively, you'll be better equipped to relax with another man.

As a bottom, it is also your responsibility to guide your top through the session. After all, it's your innards he's got his hand inside. If you feel more pain than you think should be there, ask him to slow down, or even stop the session. Practice breathing. Several men mentioned that fisting was what they thought giving birth must feel like. Think of that and recall just how much emphasis maternity wards put on breathing exercises!

Once your top has you in the sling and you're relaxing into the session, one of the most important aspects of being there is to ease yourself into the headspace. Visualize what you're expecting from the experience. Think about how good this is going to be and allow yourself to draw the top's hand into your body. As much as he has to give a little push, your body can provide a great deal of assistance by pulling. Give your top cues as well. If you feel like you want to moan with pleasure, go right ahead. It will allow the top to better read you and to also read his progress. And besides, no one likes topping a lump of wood.

The key to all of this is wanting to enjoy it. Be it from the aspect of submission in an SM scene, the desire to have the physical fullness of another man's hand inside you, or to reach a higher spiritual element through handball, more than anything else, attitude is everything. As many have said before me, the mind is still the body's best sexual organ.

FOUR: CLOSE ENCOUNTER OF THE FOOT KIND

A True Toe Tail from Moose

When I was about 24 years old, I was living in San Francisco with two guys who were lovers. They were into leather, motorcycles, BDSM, and other scenes, and had been in SF for years. They were enjoying taking me out to meet their friends and introduce me around. I was slowly getting initiated into the Folsom Street lifestyle. This was in the wild and free pre-AIDS days of the 1970s, when the bathhouses were all open and running non-stop, and no one thought about getting anything more serious than the clap. I was adventurous, and always willing to try something new. My attitude then was as it is now: don't put down anyone for what turns them on - we're all different, and if you don't try something new, you might miss out on a great, new experience.

We were at a Sunday afternoon beer bust at a bar on Castro Street that has long since closed (or morphed into something else, at least), when they introduced me to one guy I'll never forget. He was in his late 30's, average looks and average build. He had sized me up pretty quickly, as I was in shape, young, muscular, and considered good-looking. I noticed him quickly look at my feet and my hands as he approached our threesome. When Bob and Tom introduced us, I reached out to shake his hand. Now, I have always had a strong handgrip - guys still comment on it today, many years later. Anyway, when I shook his hand, he was transfixed; he kept turning our clasped hands over and over, first one way, then the next. Not in a way that was like wrestling - he just wanted to see my hands and feel them.

I gave Bob and Tom looks like, "What the hell is this idiot up to?", and they just smiled at me. The three of us talked, and the new guy went to get drinks for us all. I *had* to ask Bob and Tom what was up. "Don't you get it?" one of them asked. "He wants you to fist him!" I had never heard of fist-fucking, so this was a new one. I asked some questions about it, amazed that my hand could fit up inside another man's ass. "Yeah," said Tom, "that's why he was checking out your hands so closely - he likes guys with big hands and short fingernails - just like yours." At this time, the guy returned from the bar with drinks for all four of us, and we continued talking. I was thinking to myself that this was something new and different, and I was curious. Also, it was something that wasn't going to hurt *me*, and this guy really wanted it. I decided that if he asked me to go home with him, I would, and see what happened.

Well, it didn't take long for him to ask me to go home with him. He didn't live far away - on one of the streets that intersects Castro, maybe a block or two off it. Once in his bedroom, I was surprised to see a hotplate with a large pan of water on it sitting right next to the bed. Inside the pan of water was a large can of Crisco. Ever the naive one, I asked him, "What's this for?"

"You'll find out in a minute," he replied, turning the hotplate on. He immediately stripped down. He wasn't interested so much in me getting naked as he was in getting the water (and the Crisco) warmed up. In a few minutes of small talk, he asked me what size shoes I wear. I told him 10 1/2 D, and he said, "That's a nice, big size. Do you ever buy gloves? What size gloves do you wear?" Like most guys, I have no idea what size gloves I wear, and couldn't tell him. "Not a problem," he said. "I could tell from shaking hands with you that your hands are just the right size for me."

By then, the Crisco was warm and soft. He directed me each step of the way, telling me what to do, where to place my hand, down to clasping my fingers, etc. He laid back and spread his cheeks, placing his feet on my shoulders. I was entranced as I watched my hand disappear up this guy's rear end! It was something so far from what I was used to. But he was getting so excited, and his dick was like a lead pipe, he was so turned on. As more and more of my arm started to vanish from sight, I soon realized that there wasn't much more room up inside him to take any more of me. About half of my right arm was inside his rectum - right up to the point where the forearm muscles really begin to get bigger. I fingered his prostate when he aksed me to, and clenched my hand into a fist when he wanted it. He was in sheer ecstacy and I was amazed.

All the while he was furiously stroking his dick. Finally, he shot a huge load all over his chest, but that wasn't enough. He had me slowly pull my arm out of his backside, and, as his eyes rolled back into place, he handed me a towel to clean off my arm and hand. He got down off the bed and kneeled at my feet and started to take my boots off. First the right one, then the left. I was wearing engineer boots - my favorites, and, apparently, his favorites, too. He stopped to bury his nose deep inside each of my sweaty, stinky boots, and then licked the toe of each boot for good measure. Then, he pulled my socks off. Damp and rank, he gave them a good whiff and told me how great my feet smelled. All the time he was eyeing my now bare feet. Then he told me to lie back on the bed, propping myself up on the pillows, which I did. What happened next blew my mind.

He reached into the soft, warm Crisco and got a handful of it. He smeared the stuff all over my right foot. I just watched in silence. Then, he climbed up on the bed over my leg, spread his cheeks apart, and slowly lowered his ass down onto my foot. I always like to keep my feet looking neat, so my toenails were well trimmed and not about to rip his insides out. I'm sure he was prepared to give me a pedicure if he thought they were too long! It took a little coaxing on the part of his well-stretched sphincter muscle, but eventually he was able to get all of my toes up his ass. I have a moderately wide foot (D to E width), and a decent instep and arch, and he was really struggling to get as much of my right foot up his butt as he could. He finally got my 10 1/2 D up inside him to just about the instep. Of course, the entire time he was sporting quite the rod - and this was just minutes after shooting a huge load with my fist inside him. He started to raise up off my foot, and then sink down on it. Slowly at first, but then gradually faster and faster. He was actually fucking himself on my right foot!

At one point, he stopped and reached over the side of the bed. He grabbed one of my dirty engineer boots and started to hump my foot again. He was licking and sniffing my boot as my foot was going in and out of his asshole. I'd had some experience with dirty talk, so I started in on him, hoping it was the right thing to do. "You really like having my fucking foot up your ass, don't you, you pervert?" He moaned into my boot as he was smelling my footsweat in the boot lining. "Yeah, that's it - make love to my fucking boot." That was about all I got the chance to say - he shot another incredible load, this time all over my stomach and chest. He pulled his body off my foot and collapsed on the bed. I was stunned - I had never seen anything like that, even in a porn movie!

I was too stunned at what had just transpired to be able to get off myself. He offered to suck me off, or do whatever was necessary to coax a load out of my cock. I told him, no, it wasn't necessary. He cleaned up my right foot for me, lying on the bed with his face just inches from my left foot. He carefully wiped in between my toes, and made sure that everything was nice and neat. He was continuing to enjoy the smell of my left foot as long as he could. Then, he pulled my socks on for me, and handed me my boots. As I pulled my boots on, I thanked him for a good time and he said, "No, I am the one who should be thanking *you*! You have beautiful hands and feet, and that was a wild session!"

We exchanged phone numbers, but I never saw him again. It wasn't my last experience with fisting or footfucking, but it *was* my first for both!

A Boner Book

FIVE: PEOPLE
Club Life

About twenty men are sitting around in a small lobby area of a building located in the Philadelphia Italian Market area, relaxing on a Saturday evening. A tall, richly-voiced man is getting the activity under way for the night, giving a kind of rundown for the rules of the house. "If you're a smoker, you can go out back. But please try not to have sex talk while you're outside, because we don't want to have the neighbors hearing that kind of stuff." He gives a few more comments about the play area and the way thing are laid out, and then talks about a few added goodies for the guests. "There are frozen Crisco balls in the freezer and also frozen J-Lube tubes if you want to have a little fun with those...."

Ed Klein is the President and co-founder of the Philly Phists. Like many fisting clubs around the country, he helps set up and host parties for men with similar interests. These clubs are all over the world, and some, like the Red Hankies of San Diego (RHSD), Mid American Fists In Action (M.A.F.I.A,) the Fist Fuckers of America (F.F.A.) have an international scope. In addition to providing a safe place to play, they also serve as a nexus for fisters across the globe to share common desires.

Slings in the Philly Phists' clubhouse; photo by Tim Brough

While Ed co-founded the Philly Phists with Brad Young in September of 2000, Bill Freyer was setting the foundations for the RHSD in 1989. Creating the group predominantly because there was no other way to meet people that were into fisting, Bill decided to run an ad in the paper and see if there were any other like-minded people in the San Diego area. "I put 'FF' in the ad, saying let's get together and meet. Within a few months I had maybe ten people responding. I figured great, if I can keep this going, then maybe we can get a group going, and that is how the ball got started. Our first gathering was a social meet and greet, to get everybody together that responded to the ad. It was probably six months till we had a play party. Since then, we've grown to an average membership of around 300. That's worldwide. I've never really been a member of any other fisting groups, but I have kind of 'honorary visitor' status with them."

Ed also spoke of a need for people to find each other as a reason to start his club. "It's a way to meet other people. It's a social activity and a way to meet guys who are into what you're into. If it's fisting or any sexual activity, it's guys who have the same likes you do. It's probably better than flagging yourself at a bar. You'll probably have better luck." Besides, as Bill figures, "It's not like you can wander into a local bookstore and say 'hey, where can I go get fisted?'"

But clubs also serve as a safe haven. Bill looks from the twin points of view for health and safety issues. "There are a lot of people that are wary of having full-on sex now because of HIV, AIDS, Syphilis; you name it. With fisting, there is no actual intercourse *per se* with genitalia. It's a very safe type of sex, whether your hand is up somebody's ass or vice versa. Everybody's having a good time without doing something that would be totally unsafe. One of the major things that I've always strived for is that, if people are willing to sign their name to an application to join a club, and have a searchable avenue to track people, then the members are going to be much safer. You're not going to get a Jeffrey Dahmer in the RHSD, because the person has to submit information about himself. There's that modicum of safety as well as a sense of family. Whether you join RHSD or some other club, you feel a little more bonded towards your fellow members. It's like safety in numbers. Belonging to a club or organization that knows who its members are, if you play with somebody in the membership, then you're a safer candidate for having fun and not having to worry about being endangered. There are way too many people out there that are just crazy enough or don't know what they're doing. And they can harm someone if they don't know what they're doing."

Some members also just like the idea of a number of guys. Ed claims to have always been turned on by having a whole group of players around him "doing the things I like to do, myself! To see and hear that happening close to you is a turn on to me."

To that end, both the Philly Phists and RHSD host frequent gatherings. The Phists have their own clubhouse, and in addition to putting on regular fisting parties, Ed also plays host to a variety of other themed gatherings. These include water sports, foot nights and the occasional "anything goes" event. RHSD members travel around Southern California, meeting up for beer busts at the L.A. Faultline and play parties at the Coral Sands (a notorious motel in Los Angeles). "We still unofficially host play parties at the Coral Sands," Bill comments. "We'll just announce that RHSD will be there on a particular date; if you want to, go ahead and show up. Get your own room and do your own thing. It generates getting the fisters together on the same date."

Fortunately for the Philly Phisters, they have a real nice clubhouse. Ed enjoys the coziness of it. That "you can still have intimacy in a large group. Right now we have eight slings set up downstairs and we can set up a couple more. It's a clubhouse that's not so big that people get lost in it. People come here for the thrill of group play. A lot of guys have never been into group fisting, and many times they come here just curious. They want to see how it's different from doing it one-on-one with someone in their own bedroom."

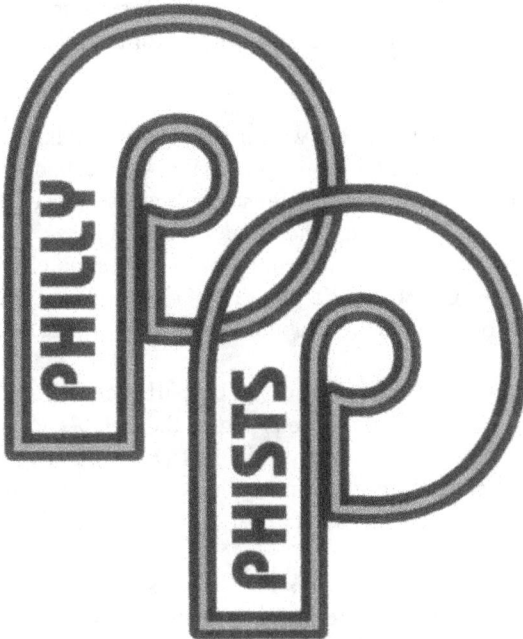

The Philly Phists' Club Logo

RSHD has also done eight Fist Fests. In its own way, it's an annual fisting convention. Fist Fest essentially takes over an entire hotel, with attendance ranging near 300 people every year, and guys coming from throughout Europe and around the globe. "They come in for anywhere from three to five days. It's a time to meet other fisters from all over the world and bond, and meet continual players year after year that you feel comfortable with." Bill adds, "Others come just for the raw debauchery that you can have from just having these men around that are willing to satisfy you in every way. But for me, personally, it's a chance for everybody to get together and just be themselves. You don't have to be afraid of someone going – *fisting! Gross!* For the most part, the serious players are there. Even the new people that show up, even if they don't get around to playing, can watch and learn from that. Overall, it's a great weekend. We set up the slings so that you can play wherever you want; out in the sun or under the stars. Sometimes you'll meet people from your own neighborhood that you didn't realize were there."

Bill did bring up a few of the hazards that organizing events like this can carry. The hotel, on the very first year, said they knew how much of a mess Crisco makes and asked if there was any other possible lube Fist Fest could use. "They're not too friendly with Crisco," Bill laughed, "because once it gets into your carpets or sheets, it's almost impossible to get out. So we make up J-Lube and pass it out to everyone who attends. It's water based, so if it gets into anything, it washes right out." He paused for a moment before adding, "Personally, I like Elbow Grease."

"Before we had the first Fist Fest, we met with CCBC. I talked to them well in advance to let them know the kind of group that we are, and told them that if they can't handle it, then we'd look for someplace else. But they just said that as long as everybody cleans up after themselves and doesn't leave too much of a mess, they were okay. But I have approached other hotels, and as soon as you say fisting or Crisco, they'd just say NO WAY! We've got the closed-minded people on that end of the community spectrum, too."

While parties and gatherings are always a big part of club life, so is education. Both Ed and Bill make that a serious part of their club's activities. Bill has gone so far as to be a participant in the Hot Desert Knights' instructional DVD, *Fisting 101*. And sitting in on the Philly Phists' basic fisting class was, as far as I am concerned, an essential part of the research for this book.

"We've had good luck with our 'Fisting 101' classes," Ed tells me. "Many of the guys have never tried fisting, and they come here with lots of concerns. Is it dangerous? Is there pain? Will their butt ever be able to function normally again? Some don't know the preparation a bottom or a top has to make before a fisting session. They come with their questions and we try to alleviate their concerns as much as we can, but we'll be honest in telling them what they're going to face. We delve into everything. Like how to meet a partner, the actual fisting, the mental part. I have always believed that fisting is more a mental act than the physical act itself. If you can connect with your partner, you can't lose. If you can get in synch with each other, you've got it made."

It's a sentiment that Bill echoes. "I teach 'Fisting 101' once or twice a year. Sometimes here in San Diego, or in Palm Springs and Los Angeles. I think, too, that a lot of people are looking for something beyond the regular vanilla. They may start playing with toys, and they want something a little bit bigger. Maybe they know about fisting and want to try it out, or they meet up with the right person at the right time, and they may be playing with their butt. All of a sudden more than a couple of fingers slip in, and they go, 'Oh! That feels good!'"

"Sometimes, if we're at an event like Leatherfest or an Orange County Leather Sampler, you'll have a dichotomy of people showing up and wanting to learn about all kinds of aspects of kink. A lot of it they may never want to try, but the more information they have, the better and more informed they feel. At an event like Leatherfest, you have all sorts of people. Straight, gay, male or female, and I've had as many as 200 people sitting in on my classes at one time. I'll have all kinds of people coming up to ask questions afterwards. When you're delivering information to that amount of people, a lot of them might be there for a different venue. They may attend a class because they may want to learn about something new, or they may have three hours free before the next seminar that they really want to attend."

Bill emphasizes that these seminars should never be considered solely for the novice. "Sometimes I get friends who have been into fisting for years and will attend one of my classes and find some aspect that they'd never realized about fisting. The most important thing I hope people get from one of my classes is that even the most experienced person can learn something new. I cover the anatomy down to where I can tell people exactly what does happen when you're being fisted, or what to expect when you're inserting the hand. Even the novice that walks into my class will easily know 90% more than what he did when he walked in. Whether he ever chooses to follow through and actually try fisting or not, at least he has the knowledge that he takes home with him."

Boasting that the membership of RHSD consistently rides above 300, Bill is expanding the club. "When I started Red Hankies of San Diego, it was primarily intended for the San Diego community. Little did I know that it would grow to the proportions that it has. So to reach out beyond that scope, we decided to start Red Hankies International. It would be a spin-off of RHSD, but at the same time, it would have its own individuality and personality. It'll have its own website with a shopping cart and membership. We also did our first video and filmed a second at Fist Fest. Bill (Gardner, of Hot Desert Knights) has been very supportive of the RHSD and in supporting Red Hankies International, and he's helping us with our DVDs."

But for my Saturday evening at The Philly Phists' clubhouse, this is a night for old-fashioned down and dirty play with the locals. In the basement of the clubhouse, all eight slings are in full use. A table in the hallway leading to the sling area is loaded with the large size cans of Crisco, plastic bowls and an ice cream scoop to dish it out without using your fingers. There's a big pile of old newspapers to lay under the sling to keep the floor from getting too greasy. A large stack of both latex and Nitrile gloves (for guys who are allergic to latex) is available, along with many rolls of paper towels for fast cleanup. I am upstairs in the kitchen area, where there is a cabinet counter covered with snacks and fresh fruits, and a fridge filled with bottled water and cans of soda, as well as a rack of toys and other accoutrements for sale. As I chat with Ed and some of the other Phisters, several guests pop up for a quick trip to the freezer. They grab a couple of the frozen Crisco balls and quickly disappear down the stairs again.

Ed chuckles. "For setting up the fisting parties, I have to make sure that everything is as clean as can be in the play area. I also get all the slings up. It's a matter of putting everything that will get used out before the party. And that includes the frozen Crisco Balls and Frozen J-Lube Tubes. They have to be put in the freezer. Early."

(Postscript: Shortly before the completion of this book, Ed announced that he would be leaving Pennsylvania. The Philly Phists held their final party in September of 2005.)

CRISCO ON THE LENS:
Bill Gardner, President of Hot Desert Knights Video

TB: How long ago did you start Hot Desert Knights?

Bill Gardner: I started it back in 1998. Our first film was released in February of 1999. It was *Bareback Buddies*. We made it in Palm Springs, where John and I were living at the time. We had no clue what we were doing, but it turned out pretty good. We made another one immediately after that called *Bareback Raunch*, and that was the first one to have fisting in it.

TB: What made you decide to put fisting into your videos?

BG: My partner and I had been into fisting for about ten years. It's something we do and we both enjoy. There aren't a lot of fisting videos out there, and many of them that are, are pretty much canned videos without a lot of emotions. We figured that's what we're into, so let's do it our way.

We started this company for fun. We didn't start it to get rich or make a lot of money, we started it for fun. We've always said we'll keep doing it as long as it is fun. So why not do fisting? That's what we do. It turned out to be a good decision.

TB: What are some of the videos you saw before you started the company that you thought of as particularly hot?

BG: A couple from Raging Stallion. But if you're asking for titles, I can't remember who made what. I remember Hot House made some really good ones early on. *Laying Pipe* was one that I watched early on and I liked it. *Doctor Goodglove*, too. They were kind of staged; that is what you see with so many of the adult videos today, whether it's fisting or not fisting. A lot of staging and a lot of non-emotion. The guys really aren't getting into it.

TB: How do you pick the people to be in yours?

BG: When we first started out, we went to Onelist.com. They were mainly lists of different groups. I belonged to various bareback and fisting mailing lists. We sent out an e-mail that said we're going to make a video. We've never done this before, and we don't know if we'll even make a dime at it, and we can't pay! But we will pay your way here; you'll get a free mini-vacation in Palm Springs. If you're interested, send us an e-mail.

I think in that first weekend, we got about 400 replies. We weeded through that and we ended up, for the first film, with nine guys, maybe ten. We spent the whole weekend filming and had a ball. We didn't have a clue as to what we were doing, but our method of filming then, as it is now, is 'you guys do what you do best and you do what feels good, and we'll do our best to stay out of your way.' Then we keep the cameras going. That's pretty much how we do it. We don't stage it; we don't have to shoot the same scene three or four times. It's just non-stop action.

TB: Is that still the criterion for your video production?

BG: Yes. We always use a minimum of two cameras, and since this past year, we've been using three. We have a close-up camera and a compact camera that moves around and catches facial expressions. Then we have a third camera that catches all the action, including the cameraman getting the shots and what he has to do in order to get them. For the most part, we can go nonstop, and know when we come back for the editing process, we're going to have all the action that we need and we haven't missed anything. We can edit back and forth to catch facial expressions and that sort of thing. We don't lay any music tracks on most of our films. We want the real sounds, the moans and the groans and the 'ah fucks,' those kinds of things.

I filmed a video one time called *Dungeon Fuck Party,* and we did *Dungeon Fist Party*. None of these guys were what you'd call professional actors. This was one of the few occasions that we only used one camera for each. I was doing the fist party; the fact that we only had the one camera forced me to make sure that I not only got the action shots, seeing the hand going in or the two hands, but also forced me to make sure that I got the facial shots. So, many of the shots I was taking were over the top's shoulder. I could see the bottom's face as he was lying in the sling or on his knees, and you could just tell how much he was enjoying it. We got more comments written to us about that video than on any fisting video we've ever done. The letters said they really enjoyed watching the bottom enjoying himself and watching his facial expressions. They also really enjoyed watching the top. I was going around and shooting over the bottom's shoulder and shooting towards the top, and catching the expressions that he was making. You could just tell that they had eye-to-eye contact the entire time and were really going at it. It turned out to be one of the best fisting videos we've ever made and one of the most popular.

TB: What do you think makes a video hot?

BG: I think intensity and the realness of the actors, that they're not just acting, that they're actually getting into what they're doing, and it feels good to them. The models need to be able to relate to each other, and that's a big thing.

What we do is bring all the models in that are going to be in the filming. The filming on some of the productions may take up to a week. The first night, we all go out to dinner together, we all get to know each other, and we'll go to a bar and buy a round of drinks for everybody. Then my partner and I will sit off to the side and watch who is interacting with who. We may already have a preconceived notion of whom we want in a scene, based on looks. But then when we see how they're interacting with each other, we almost always change it.

TB: Anyone ever formed a partnership out of acting for you?

BG: I know they have, in the first video! There were two guys that met during *Bareback Buddies* and they're still together. They live in Long Beach. Same thing on the second film, and they now live in San Diego.

TB: What was the first Hot Desert Knights film that was exclusively aimed at fisting?

BG: Exclusively, it was probably *Fist Pigs*. But prior to that, we shot a dungeon scene called *Hole Hunters* that ended up being 60 or 70 percent fisting. The action just kind of naturally migrated into that. But *Fist Pigs* was the very first one that was strictly going to be a fisting video. We filmed that in early 2000. We followed it up with *Fist Pigs 2*, because it turned out so successfully.

TB: You've also produced *Fisting 101*, which is quite possibly the only fisting instructional video in existence.

BG: I think it is. I don't think anyone else has done a fisting 101 like we did. In fisting, it always seemed like it was older guys. The younger guys were really not into fisting, then as they matured, then they began to discover new worlds. Fisting became one of those worlds. But today, there are more and more younger guys. We were getting a lot of e-mails from our customers that had never been fisted, and this was the first time they'd ever seen it. They were asking lots of questions about it, and that's how *Fisting 101* came about.

TB: What is Hot Desert Knights' biggest seller?

BG: It wouldn't be a fisting title. The fisting community is a smaller community, so our best selling title is probably one of our regular fuck videos. Then our second best is *Jeff Palmer Hardcore.* That one is an orgy/dungeon set thing that was probably about 75% fisting.

TB: Did you have video experience before you started Hot Desert Knights?

BG: I owned a company that was involved in the transportation/safety industry for ten years prior to starting Hot Desert Knights. We made transportation/safety videos and sold them all over the United States. I did really well with that, and sold the company and retired to Palm Springs. The way we got into making the adult videos that we make today is because we were having sex parties at our house. After the second or third party, it was probably three or four o'clock in the morning and we were sitting around drinking a beer or smoking a cigarette, winding down. Someone said 'you guys used to make videos, didn't you?' And I said yes, and he said, 'well, why don't you make fuck videos?'

I replied because we never thought about it. Then, of course, for the next three weeks, all I did was think about that. So I thought, what the hell. We've got the know-how, we've got the equipment. Why not do it? That's how the first one came about, actually.

TB: How early did you make the jump to DVD?

BG: We went almost exclusively to DVD last year. We still have some VHS available. Our business has grown, the complexity of it, substantially. When we first started out, it was 100% to the retail market, and strictly online. Now about 65% of our sales are wholesale. We sell all over Europe and Australia now, and you always had the problem overseas that you had to have the PAL code, and DVD has eliminated that. We do everything in-house and the DVD's are code-free. We do our own editing, encoding, replication, we print the disc ourselves, shrink-wrap. Nothing goes out other than the printing of the covers.

We own two companies. We have Hot Desert Knights, Inc., which is the production company. We don't film in California anymore. We also own another company called HDK distribution. That's the distribution wing of the corporation, and they are in Palm Springs. I'm not as involved in the distribution as I used to, since I moved to the East Coast for my supposed semi-retirement, though I talk to the office every day. By being here on the east coast, we're very close to Philadelphia, Baltimore, DC, New York City.... there's a wealth of opportunities here to do some filming.

TB: When you prepare to get a video shoot together, what are some of the first things you do?

BG: We decide what kind of video we're going to make; is it going to be a fuck video or a fisting video? After that point, we start looking at the model applications that we have on hand. Then, if we don't have the models we think we want for that particular film, we start looking out in the industry and find guys to be in it.

TB: Say, if we focused on the fact that you were going to make a fisting video, what would you look for other than willingness to fist or be fisted?

BG: Well, that would be the primary thing we'd be looking for. But our philosophy has always been that we don't want a bunch of shaved Adonises. We don't ever want to be a Falcon or a Catalina, we want average guys that we can relate to. If you ran into them at a bar at one o'clock in the morning, you could relate to the person. You wouldn't be afraid to walk up and try to strike up a conversation. We're looking for average guys that are really into fisting, and can do unusual things. Like they could take it to the shoulder, they can take it to the elbow, they can take two hands, they like getting punched, so we're not coming out with a vanilla fisting video.

We came out with one not too long ago that was filmed down in Texas. It's a group of guys that get together a couple times a year and have big fisting parties. They're all really good friends and they all know what turns each other on. And they all love fisting. We just went down there and basically turned on the cameras and said, 'ok guys, go at it!' It was a little tough editing the damn thing because there was so much action going on all at the same time. But man, we got some unbelievable shots. One guy, honest to God, did take it up to the shoulder. It's called *Chris Cohand's Pigs Gone Wild*.

Bill Feyer, the president of Red Hankies Of San Diego, just started a new company called Red Hankies International. They've started making videos and we're helping with them. They shot their first one, and then we helped with the filming and editing. We just released that as *Chris Cohand's Gang Bang Rodeo*. That was also shot in Houston at the same place. It was western themed, they all had red scarves, cowboy hats and boots, but they do unusual things. They're all such good friends that they can get away with it. The camaraderie that really exists there comes through on the film, so you see that they're having a damn good time.

TB: How many hours of film do you think you get per shoot?

BG: For each scene we're probably going through five to six hours per scene, and you've got four scenes per video. So you're looking at 24 to 25 hours of film per video. We'll edit this down to between 90 and 120 minutes. I probably then spend 200 hours editing this down to the final cut. I know there are a lot of companies that can whip it out in two or three days, but if you look at their product, that's what it looks like, I think. We really take our time in editing. There are several people involved and it gets looked at a lot, but there's only one editor. Changes get made, things get cut...it's a long, drawn-out process.

TB: When you're editing, what to you constitutes a "keeper?"

BG: The intensity of it, something that's real or something that's unusual. Let me give you an example. We were filming a fuck video called *Cum Hungry*. In one of the scenes, we were underneath the action when the top cums. He pulls out of the hole and he shoots, then he shoves it back in, and the cum is dripping everywhere. Then you actually see it falling off the bottom's butt and hitting the camera lens in two different places. We knew, right then, that was a keeper because it was so damned unusual. We were lucky, because it hit right on the outside edges of the lens. The viewer gets to see that happening. He sees it dripping down and then finally falling and splattering right on the camera. But the center of the lens was as clear as it could be the whole time.

Let me tell you about one that I didn't get to keep. I'll probably regret this and I am not going to tell you who it was or what film it was for, but we edited it out. We had the bottom on his knees and this top that's got a really big dick. He's got this bottom pressed up against the wall and he is ramming his cock up there, and I mean all the way in. This guy's got like a nine or ten inch dick. He's really going at it, and the bottom is taking it all, I mean, he's a trouper. But all of a sudden he's starting to gag and choke, and then the bottom stops the action and pushes the top away. I forget who, but someone yelled 'cut.' We cut the cameras, and it turned out the bottom had false teeth and the top had rammed them down the guy's throat! I'll always regret that we didn't keep the cameras going and that we couldn't have put that in some kind of blooper reel. We haven't done a blooper reel yet, but we sure have enough footage.

TB: I guess that falls under the category of 'always tell the top about what problems you may have!' How do you choose a location?

BG: People sometimes offer; that's how this thing happened in Houston. Up until the last year or so, we had our own studio in Palm Springs. But due to the regulations in California, we quit that and sold it. We had a 2,000 square-foot dungeon and studio there, and we could film just about anything. We had the dungeon on one side, we had the bedroom set up on the other, and a living room set up where we could change out pictures and couches and lamps, and that kind of stuff.

Now as far as outside work, we shot one video at Inn Leather in Fort Lauderdale. But for the most part, when you're shooting a fisting video, you want it to be a little hard-core, a little leathery, and a little dungeon-like. We shot off-location a lot for regular fuck videos; Key West, Fort Lauderdale, Phoenix, but not so much for the fisting. Most of them were shot in our own dungeon, or if someone had a large playroom set-up, we've gone there to film.

TB: Then just turn the actors loose?

BG: We have a rough script. We sit down with them and say 'here's what we're thinking.' We'll run that by the guys, and if there's something they can't or don't want to do, then we don't do it. We give them that rough idea, then we tell them, if while you're playing and he starts doing something that we haven't mentioned, you're really getting into it and it's feeling good, then just keep it going and don't worry about us. Sometimes the best laid plans of men and mice just go to shit.

I mean, we did a scene the other day that (starts laughing) - oh my god. We ended up with maraschino cherries and whipped cream and bananas....it was the damndest thing you ever saw. But it's a hot, hot, very intense scene. This is what *they* wanted to do. I mean, they didn't tell us! They just showed up, these two guys that knew each other and had played together quite a bit, and they just wanted to do something really hot and different. That's what they ended up doing, basically one making a banana split in the other one's butt. There were some water sports involved, too.

I'm normally the one shooting the close-up shots, and in most cases that means I'm only about a foot away. I was starting to get a little nervous about where the hell all this whipped cream was going to go. It tuned out to be pretty hot!

TB: C'mon, it's whipped cream. How much dirtier can that be than Crisco?

BG: There's nothing worse than Crisco. We have to get special lenses to go *on* our lenses. While we're filming the action, I'm down there, eight, nine inches away from it, and if he slaps a butt, that Crisco just goes everywhere. Instead of stopping the action, all I have to do is just screw off this lens and screw on a clean one. I've got a guy standing behind me with several clean ones to change them real quick.

TB: Aside from the food festival there, what would you say would have been the most intense, spontaneous moment that you've captured on film?

BG: That would have been a three-way in *Hole Hunters* that we had with one Daddy and two boys. The scene started off on a motorcycle, and the top just *used* those two bottoms. It was totally spontaneous, we had no idea how it was going to go and he just really worked them over good. It had a tremendous amount of water sports in it. Also turned out to have a hot fisting scene in it that none of us knew was going to happen. The guy that got fisted had never been fisted before. But Daddy Ken was able to get it in, and it was unbelievable.

TB: For guys like that first-timer, what would you tell them if they were curious about fisting?

BG: What I tell guys is that if they like being fucked, they will love being fisted, as it is 100 times more intense and pleasurable. But fisting can also be dangerous. Never set goals, never say that on 'so and so date I am going to take my first fist.' All you do is either set yourself up for disappointment or risk injury if you try to go too fast.

Take it slow and easy, and always play with an experienced top. He'll know what to do, when to do it, and when you are ready. Fisting is more in your mind than it is in your ass. Just take it easy, go slow, enjoy what is happening, and let it take its natural course.

Hands Across The Internet:
Lee William Klement – RedRightweb Online

It was one good session. I knew it was gonna be, that's why I gave the camera to a buddy and said, "Shoot until you get bored." This top and I, we had a thing. His arm, my ass — it's some kind of perfect fit. We play and it's magic. His entry is so smooth, I barely know he's gone in. In a minute he tickles my second ring and then he's doing the long slide, his whole forearm gliding into my ass. I feel the stretch before the elbow, take a hit of poppers, and it's done - his elbow's buried in my ass. This is just the warm-up.

I think what attracts me to fisting over other kinds of sex is that it's hard sex. To me, it's absolutely the most masculine kind of sex. There's an element of risk, of edginess. It always comes back to the intensity of the experience.

I'm a bottom if I can get away with it. There is a community of fisters, and it's a very coherent community. There are fisting organizations, fisting parties. Because of my time in it, and that my lifestyle allows me to travel, and my website allows me to make connections, I have been to fisting parties in as far-flung places as London, Seattle, New York, and it's amazing how there's this common etiquette. At a party like that, it's better manners to switch than to be all bottom or all top. Also, in a one-on-one situation with a fellow fister, unless they have a stated preference to be all bottom or all top, it's considered more mannerly and to have good grace to be a switch.

He rolls his arm with the elbow inside and rocks my world — sends me rocketing into outer space. He pulls the arm out a little and gives me the thrill of the elbow popping out again. In, out, in, out — each slide over the elbow is like an orgasm. Next, he starts giving me a real stretch, adding his other hand to the deeply-buried first. Deep breaths, a little poppers and we do that too. Two hands stuffing my ass — heaven, wide, deep heaven. How deep? How wide? He explores where my ass can go with two hands. Two arms. It goes far.

Our community exists in no small part due to the seminal role of Bert Herrman, the author of *Trust* (Alamo Square, 1991) and his *Trust Newsletters*. There's one other book that's out of print and rare, called *Purusha; The Divine Androgyne* (Sanctuary, 1981), which was completely spiritual and more than a little wacko. An enjoyable read; I have a copy myself, carefully wrapped and put away. I have great admiration for what Bert achieved. It was the *Trust Newsletter* that got me from fisting once in a very great while to something that is a regular part of my life.

I get feedback like that now from my website, when they find out who I am, and tell me that RedRightWeb got me into the scene. I first put the site up ten years ago. It was just months after joining the company that I work for that I got myself a real internet connection, realized that the connection came with web space, and thought "what can I do with that?" Since my favorite kind of porn is the written word, and fisting stories are few and far between, I had started to wear out my magazines. I was too shy to take them down to Kinko's and copy them, so I typed them up.

I had all these text files of fisting stories on my computer. It was a very short hop to take those and make a website out of them. I put up the stories, and people started sending me photographs. I was not that interested in them at the time, since photographs on the Internet were pretty slow then. I just dumped them into a directory. People could click on the file name and see the photo. That was the initial version of my website.

The stories had HTML pages, and the photos were a big pile of stuff that people could rifle through. There weren't any thumbnails or anything like that. I got curious as to how many people were visiting my website, and since I am a computer geek, I wrote some scripts to count my numbers everyday. Somebody hacked me about three years into the website's life and rewrote that script so that the last thing the script would do was erase the entire website. I did have backups, and had it back online within a month. Now, if someone was going to do that, I decided to comeback bigger and better. So the website that you see today is a result of my getting hacked, and then wanting to do a better version of it.

Then one hand slips away and it's back to depth again. Deep and deeper. He takes me places we haven't been before. I feel like I must be almost to his shoulder. Our rhythm is perfect and I want it to go on forever. In time, some limit is reached. We both feel it. He starts to pull back from the extreme depth and I know this is the last slide out. "Make it slow," I urge him. He does. I feel every inch of his long arm as he slowly pulls out. Every inch. It's like silk sliding through my guts. Ecstasy.

From there, I progressed and got more into a relationship with someone and my job got more intense. I kept getting feedback that I love your website, and your website has done good things for me. So I kept it up, and I get the space for a ridiculously low fee. But it's a slow project that I do with the little spare time that I have. I often tell people that, given the choice between sitting behind my computer and working on the website or getting an arm up my butt, I'll take the arm.

I searched out links, carefully. It wasn't just everything I could come up with. It was organizations I had confidence in and a high opinion of. It was the one thing I hoped would set my website apart from everyone else's. It's not going to be every fisting photograph I can get my hand on, it's got to be stuff that turns me on. The stories have to pass the standard that they'll make me cum before they get up there.

Finally he's out. My butt feels so empty. It's heartbreak, it's elation, it's satiation, it's hunger. He holds his arm up for me to see the ring. Deep. Way deep. His arm glows. The photographer snaps his last shot. Ninety minutes, seventy shots — boredom never caught him. It was one good session.

SIX: INTERVIEWS

Tim in Michigan

"Fisting is to fucking as worshipping cock is to giving a blow job ..."

I did a fair amount of research and interviews in the almost yearlong gathering of resources for this book. The majority were done at events throughout 2005. Although bits and pieces of them have been interwoven through the chapters, I really felt it was worth putting some of the best and most quotable responses here. As a reminder, each person was asked to respond – at the very least – to these two questions.

What is it that most attracts you to fisting?
Can you describe for me your most memorable fisting experience?

Thanks to all who took the time to respond.

John

Basically, the most important thing is the smile on the bottom's face when my fist and arm are up his ass. I'm able to work it up in there; I've got a big hand, it's about nine inches around, and I've got nice, thick arms. When I go inside a bottom's hot ass, it turns me on to watch him smile, and knowing that my hand and my fist and arm are inside his ass. I'll be working over his prostate and, the biggest thrill is, last couple of times I got a guy that likes it, I know that I can stick my cock up in there and jerk off. And he just goes absolutely apeshit, with my hand moving and my cock in his ass, he just goes crazy.

I've been doing this for over ten years. Some guys I can get my hand in, some guys will take more, and I've got one guy that I'm able to go clear up to my elbow. Then there's another guy that I can put both my hands in his ass. His ass is like a Hoover vacuum cleaner. So for me, the most memorable was when I did my boy for the first time. He's been able to take my cock with no problem. Mostly we fuck. He came with me once to a session where I fisted other guys, and he said, "Man, I don't know, your hand's so big." He was scared to death. I said, "well, let's see how far we can go." We went on vacation, a quiet place in the country, and spent the whole time naked. It took us about a week and we worked on it. Every time we were near each other, I had one, two, three or four fingers up his ass. I just kept working and working at it, and he just kept on opening more and more. Finally, he had my hand. The look on his face when he realized that my whole hand was up his ass was pure delight for me. I said, "Are you in pain? Does it hurt," and he said, "The feeling I have is indescribable." He said he didn't think that anything that big would fit there.

We continued that week and he was able to take over half my arm, that's about 18 inches, up his ass. The last night we were on vacation, he wanted me to try and put my cock in there, too. I did, and then I started jacking off. He turned every shade of red, blue, green, purple, that you can imagine. While I was still in there, he came four times in 20 minutes. He was covered with cum from head to foot. And then, after I jacked off of in his ass, I pulled my fist out and left my cock up there, and then I gave him a piss enema. He was in seventh heaven then. I think that was the most memorable time I've ever had because he was someone who I love, who loved me back. This wasn't some trick who knew that I was able to fist people. We've only done it a couple of times since, 'cause he's still getting used to it. But he is so loving and so caring that, when it happens, he just goes crazy, and it makes me feel good. Then when we're done, we just wrap around in each other's arms and we can sleep for hours. It's the most wonderful feeling in the world.

PTownTop

The thing I like most about it is the element of trust between the top and the bottom. Watching the bottom's expression as the hand goes in, reading subtle signals as to whether to push harder or back off. It is a very intimate sex act, much more than a fuck. I'll tell you one thing. About 20 years ago, I had a boy who wanted it and I had never done it. I had a top friend and asked him to fist me, so I could learn how to do it and what it felt like before I tried to do the boy. For a 100% top to try that kind of says what I am all about. Hurt like hell, too.

DomDinosour

To go in the bathroom, give yourself an enema, come downstairs and throw your legs in the air is not foreplay! What kind of foreplay do you use when you're fisting? What do you use for foreplay if you want to take him on a mental trip? If I am just going to be a mechanic and fist him, then I'm not going to get anything out of it. Secondly, I'm not going to do a good job of fisting if I can't read him. I have to read where he is emotionally and physically. I want them to be verbal, without being a demanding bottom. They want it a certain way, because that is the way each bottom is built. You've got to find that, because if you don't, it's not good for them. And if it's not good for the bottom, it's not good for me. I want him to come back. I want to get a repeat performance out of him.

It definitely has a sense of intimacy with the other person. In my case, I am not inflicting pain, I am inflicting pleasure; a very, pardon the pun, deep pleasure. It is a sense of control with the other person. It is a real sense of involvement with him, because when my fist is up his ass, he is totally vulnerable. Therefore, he has expressed extreme trust, the deep intimacy, personal exposure and intimacy of himself. From this I feel reassured in my own sexuality, that I am attractive enough to him that he is willing to accept this exchange. There is a sense of renewal and reassertion every time. I know that my partner is in his own world, to get himself off, but as I am fisting him, he is with me. He is aware of himself physically and the presence of my fist. That is a gift of trust and sharing. There is a psychological sense of renewal during this and not always involving orgasm. It recharges me.

His act of surrender to the cross and the bondage that I use in fisting is the beginning of that bonding, that trust. But then, having submitted, I am driving him deeper into his own subconscious with the erotic pain of the flogging. His loss of control to me is starting there. That is both giving me his trust and losing his control to me, and at the same time, building up his endorphins on his back. Not marking him; I'm not doing a violent flogging, I am doing a stimulating flogging. While I have to admit, 500 strokes, however gentle, tend to get a little heavy just by the sheer number and volume and the lack of stopping! You can build on it, softly, and it will be just as painful and erotic. You can build these endorphins, which will create his whole erotic sense to himself. Then he's virtually in a ready state of collapse when I take him off the cross and pop him in the sling. He's just ready to spread his legs and take it.

There has to be an exchange. Being verbal during the fisting, during the bondage or flogging, that is OK with me. Once, at the DC Eagle during the seventies, there was some asshole who was fisting everybody and sending them to the hospital, and one of his victims had to have a colostomy. That wasn't fisting. That was sadism and abuse. One of my friends was the *fifth* person sent to the hospital needing a colostomy. While being repaired, we made it a point to spread the word about the dangerous guy.

The first time I met someone who wanted me to fist him was 1974, in New York City, in a gay church! After the service, I was cruising this man. In those days there were only two bandanas, red and blue. I was really only into the scene for about a year and was still very confused about things, signal-wise. In my case, I had a red bandana in my left pocket, not realizing that I might be scaring guys away, and I might've been better off with a blue bandana! After services, this guy took me home and I learned that there was fisting. Then I discovered that it was a whole 'cult' of sorts. As soon as I moved to Germany, I met a whole bunch of people who really wanted to get fisted. It was easier to find men at that stage, the early 80's, in Germany than America. When I came back to DC in the 90's, the FFA was there. I was invited to a couple FFA meetings. I discovered that, within the group, they were pretty well partnered up. I was invited because I was on Connecticut Avenue and ran into one of the officers of the club. He was young, horny and liked the looks of my hands! But he was partnered, so I ended up at the party with both partners, one on each hand all the way, making love to each other. They had their hands free to play with each other, while my hands were certainly not free. I couldn't touch myself, and they tended to forget about me while in this mad passionate love scene between the two of them while riding my hands! I found it to be a memorable, if very frustrating, experience.

Anonymous

My most memorable session was being fisted after a subspace whipping, with both holes filled, ass and mouth. This took place in 1980, in an outdoor setting at a private beach at night by a fire. It was my passage from being an owned slave under a two-year contract, to owning a slave. Two days of 'last call' use of me, really. Nothing has come close to matching it since then. As a Master, the experience has helped me as a trainer. I learned the absolute surrender, which was important for me to understand the mind of a slave, and to discover the route to endorphins without using chemical stimuli. I learned to displace emotion, and become more efficient at reading and listening to the slave as I fist him.

Brad

I came of age into fisting in Chicago during the early eighties when M.A.F.I.A. was getting going. I moved to Chicago, was young, attractive and competitive in the arena of hot sex and good looks. But I figured out pretty quick, especially as a blind person, that I'd better have a Plan B here when the looks went and I wasn't twenty-something. I found fisting and kink in general to be more competency based. It was what you were into and your ability with the scene that people valued and judged you by. I could compete in that arena pretty effectively. I found that to be very attractive. I found the guys and the ethic attractive. The term 'fuck buddy' was not a pejorative. You developed these very warm and intimate relationships. You not only had this commonality of shoving hands up each other's ass, and God knows what else, but when you were done, you had this network of buddies. There was a collegiality and conviviality to the whole thing that just wasn't there in the Disco scene. I think we've lost some of that in the fisting community. I won't go on about the effects of the Internet and all that, but when I came of age, to me, that community was really critical. After you pulled off the glove and wiped off the grease, that there was still something for later. So what I really got out of it was not just a sex act. I think it's incredibly intimate to go up and get inside another person, but more so the intimacy that surrounds the men you're doing it with.

The first time I went up to my elbow with some guy, we were in Man's Country. At that time it was very active, probably around 1984 or '85. The guy was in a sling and he was a hot guy. So I started to play with him, and I kept going in and going in, and he kept wanting to know how deep I was. I wouldn't tell him, because I knew once I did, he'd clamp it off. I finally got up to my elbow, and it was a first time for each of us.

I've opened guys for their first times on several occasions, the first time I help someone achieve a limit, and it's been my great honor and privilege to do that. I trust that those people also remember it. I think that those mutual firsts are what really makes it hot.

Master Darwin

Fisting? It is being inside of a person. It is having those sensitive digits up inside of a person, where you're actually linked. Me, having the devious mind that I have, I enjoy turning a masculine guy into a fucking, literal pussy. Opening his shithole up, and making him into a big pussy. Getting my hand in there, and maybe my dick, too. But I don't consider it a prelim to fucking.

In the late seventies in San Francisco, there was a converted hotel that had become a weekend sex club. One room in there had a pair of bunk beds. I proceeded one evening to start fisting this guy who obviously wanted it very badly. I hadn't had a lot of experience at that point. A crowd developed; we were on the top bunk. While I was fisting his ass, another guy came up and wanted me to fist him with my other arm. So I proceeded to give everybody a nice show of fisting both of these guys at the same time. Probably the aspect that I had so many people watching and I was giving a little bit of a performance there, made it a turn on for all of us.

In '87, I was living in Long Beach. There was a gay bar not too far from my house. Someone had graffitied a phone number outside the bar saying, "call me and stick your hand up my ass." I actually called the phone number and got two guys. It was an older guy and a younger guy, Daddy and boy. They invited me over, and I spent the whole night over there fisting his boy while his Daddy watched and participated. It got deeper and more intense as the night went on. He just opened up and opened up! He started by letting me in him, then we got into some hot fist fucking. But then we sort of grew into it and it felt like my hand was where it should be. For the bottom, it feels like the hand is where it should be, too. It's there and feeling like it's part of you.

I prefer a black leather glove. I like the natural feel of things. Being in the medical field, I wear rubber gloves all day. So I like the feeling of skin on my skin. I keep my nails clipped short and always watch for any cuts I have on my hands. Positioning is kind of key, for both parties. Certainly a sling is the most optimum position because it affords both comfort and accessibility.

Mike

I first found out about fisting in the seventies. There was a novel that I don't remember the name of that had a fisting scene in it, and I became very interested. I first fisted as a top. But then I became more interested in bottoming. I worked at it for three years, and then it just happened. My most recent fisting was my most memorable, and I've only been fisted about a dozen times to twenty. Two guys, one that I trusted a lot and who first opened me up, and the other guy, who was very hot. Brad went right into my butt, way easier than I've ever been entered before. The other guy, Dennis, was playing with my tits and kissing me. It was so good that I just wanted Brad in more and deeper. I just wanted to feel his hand turning in my butt, which he did. It just went on like that. It was like I was insatiable, and I couldn't get enough! We probably went on for over an hour, which was by far the longest fisting I've been able to take at one time.

Ed Klein – Philly Phisters

Most people know what the bottom gets out of fisting, but what does the Top get out of it? The one thing that I get out of it most is getting my partner into the space he wants to be. That makes my job rewarding. There are other parts of it; as they say, the journey is the most fun, getting there is the most fun.

I've been fisting for close to 25 years, and I've had moments where I've fisted two men at once. To have my hands in two different butts at the same time, and have them each reach orgasms at the same time. Even though I don't like to set goals, it is always a treat to get farther than you've gotten with anyone before. That's always a little kick. That happens from time to time but not too much anymore. All the places I've been around the country and I've fisted in! Oftentimes it's just the position we were fisting in. It doesn't always have to be in a sling or on a bed. It can be someone sitting down on your arm while you're lying on the floor. Or upside down, or having them in a place where they're not accustomed to being fisted. Like in a car, a kitchen table or on a mountaintop. Places that you wouldn't consider a normal place to do it.

Eric Lawrence

What attracts me to fisting ? The intimacy and actually having someone inside of me or to be inside of someone's body. That exchange of energy is fabulous. The sensations that are happening are so great.

The most memorable fisting scene has to be the time I was giving a fisting class and I had someone fist me as a demo. The moment we started, there was an intense eye contact, it was as if we had climbed into each other's body. As he entered, the energy grew; once his entire fist was in me the room lit up as my top chakra opened. It was as if we were floating together connected. I couldn't believe this was happening in the middle of a class. The rest of the class could feel the energy as the room filled with ours, and it was as if they were floating with us.

Alan

It's really kind of hard to say, because there's just so many emotions involved. Part of it is a sense of surrender; part is a sense of fulfillment. It's a very erotic feeling, very sensual; it's really just a very pleasurable feeling to do that. It's very, extremely intimate. So I think in a lot of ways, there's a connection that you get with the other person.

Well, that was the first time, actually. I didn't know it was going to happen. And it was with somebody — we had been meeting and playing around and he was just doing some ass play. All the time we had just been playing around and stretching and everything, then all of a sudden, before I knew it, he had actually stuck his hand up my ass. I didn't know he was going to try to do that, didn't know that was his intention, it was just something that happened. And it caught me by surprise, but I was pretty amazed that it had happened.

Duane

It had been a long week at work and I wanted to just relax, but I got talked into meeting friends for drinks that Friday night. I arrived earlier than they did and got talking to the bartender, who I had come to know well and liked. He was a short, slender, but muscular guy. When my friends arrived, we got caught up in having a good time and goofing off. The bartender had gotten off duty and brought me a drink and we started talking. He said he had wanted to be taken by me for a long time and was willing to play that night. My friends kept telling me to forget him and not bother, but there was something about how he was honest about it. After a few hours, I got bored with what was going on, so I asked him what he wanted done to him. He said about anything I wanted, as long as I fisted him deep by the end of the night.

I asked him just what I could do to him, and said I can get very rough and wild when given the chance. He just said good, finished his drink, and said "let's go." His place was nice. I saw his booze on the counter, so I fixed a drink and sat on the couch waiting for him. When he came back out, he was naked, a cock and ball separator on and nothing else. He came over and knelt between my legs. I reached out and played with his tits hard, twisting and pulling on them; he moaned and smiled. Then I placed a hand on the back of his neck and forced his face down to my boots. He just started licking and sucking them, I said "Good boy, too bad I don't have a crop." He just said "Sir, yes Sir" and crawled on hands and knees into the other room. He came back with a nice leather strap in his mouth.

When he got to me, he knelt with his hands behind back and leaned forward so I could take the strap out. I took it and began to run it across his face and down his chest. He was getting harder, and his cock was dripping precum. I held the strap under his cock head and got some on the end, so I made him lick it off. I then slapped it lightly across his face and ordered him down on my boots again. As he did boot worship, I began to hit his back and ass with the strap, and as it got harder and harder, he moaned and groaned and begged for more. I ordered him to present his ass to me; he turned and did so. I then slowly began slapping it harder to get it nice and red. I then said, "Let's get serious" and made him crawl on his stomach to the other room, which turned out to be his bedroom. He had one of those big waterbeds with a canopy of mirrors; also at the foot of the bed was a chain with wrist shackles hanging from it. I pulled him to his feet and attached him to his shackles.

He had put out a lot of toys, and they were spread out on top of a low dresser. I noticed a pair of leather gloves and tried them on. They were tight, but I could wear them well. I turned and began playing with his tits hard again; he groaned loudly and was panting. He was rock hard, and was well hung for a small guy; I grabbed his balls and squeezed hard. He begged for me to take him, I just smiled and said I would in my own good time. He was still dripping precum, so I coated the fingers of one glove and forced him to suck it off as I played with his balls. I started feeling and squeezing his nice round ass, and he gyrated back against my hands. I told him now we would see just how many of the dildos he could handle to their bases. I began with a small one, making him suck it and get it wet first, and then forced it in slowly and steadily. He took it all and pushed hard against it, and kept saying "more please more."

I grabbed some lube and stroked my hard cock and coated it and then said "try this one." I shoved it in to my balls and waited. He began to ride and squirm on it, until he realized it was my cock and not a dildo and really began squeezing and working it. I reached around and began working his tits as I fucked him. He said "rougher, harder *please*!" I grabbed his waist and went to town on his hot hole. He was a hot fuck for sure; he kept up with me and said to open him up for fisting. I spread-eagled him face up on bed, tied his wrists to the headboard and legs up to the chain. I grabbed the Crisco and positioned myself between his raised legs. Now I told him "time to ride" and to open up for my fist. I worked all the dildos in him from the smaller to the largest. He thrashed around begging for more and more, when he was open and ready, I began working my fist into him, glove and all. He went wild. That has to be the best one.

Jay

Not only the sensation, but the feeling, the trust factor of knowing that the person that you're having the fisting experience with is in tune with you, knows your eye gestures and your body movements, what he's doing and where he's going, to be able to release that total trust and have that confidence in him that he's not going to make a wrong gesture—he knows where to go. The body anatomy is basically simple, but a lot of people have a tendency of wanting it too fast. If they're a good top, they'll know that it takes time. Once you have that time and that patience and that trust, you can go places you could never imagine.

I guess my most memorable session was probably when I turned 31. It was my birthday, and I had a group of friends who knew what I liked; and I kind of hadn't been a bottom long in the fisting aspect of it, and I kind of mentioned that I had been practicing with the toys and getting ready for it, then just hadn't found anybody I could trust. They ended up finding somebody for me and tying me up for a wonderful birthday present. So that had to be the most memorable, because I was really into it. My two best friends were there and I was able to experience it with them. It was pretty intense. It was probably the best fisting scene I've ever been a part of. We're still friends, and we still coach each other. That's even better.

Tim Hamilton

It's fun. It's also the most intimate thing I think that I've experienced so far. And I can think back to the first time I fisted somebody. I was eighteen; it was by accident, and after about an hour I looked down and saw my wrist just gone and his body arching. From my lack of knowledge, I immediately turned my hand, which now was up to my wrist. He screamed, and I was like, *this is really something*. Twenty years later, in my thirties and forties, is when I really started exploring it. I'm not one of those punchers, where you go in and out a lot; it's the act of getting in there for me. Then maybe feeling around and feeling the heartbeat, feeling them. That's what I get out of it, an enormous sense of intimacy.

I would say my most memorable was teaching a boy who had never done it before as to what it was going to be like. I took his hand and started putting it in me and he was terrified. By the time we were done and it was in there, he looked down and tears came down his eyes. He said 'no one's ever trusted me like this before.' That just meant a ton to me, that meant a lot because he went from the erotic, which was great, and the sexual, which was great, but more that he really saw it as somebody really trusting him, and wanting to literally take part of them into themself.

Parker Perry, Waxer

There was this one Inferno. I'd been out of fisting and I was just getting back into it, and there was one guy that was absolutely gorgeous. I just went, "you'd enjoy my ass." And the second was with the best fister I've ever been with, and it was instantly like he knew everything. I never said one word. He knew when to be in and when to be out, and everything just perfect. Both the same year. Same Inferno. Same hands.

James Prock

It's the spirituality of it. There are guys who just like to be fisted. To me they're not any fun. They're just guys that don't care who's fist it is. Then there are guys that you work with, and when you finally can achieve it, it's a very special moment. If the guy considers it also, it can be a very, well, I don't want to overdo it, but it can be an experience where you have achieved something together, you worked to bear it and the final moment has been achieved.

My most memorable was this guy I had tried to fist and it didn't work, so we just kind of gave up on it, and I didn't think it would go any further. Then he called me back and we did it again, and we worked at it, although I didn't think it was going to happen. I've got some large knuckles, and that always seems to get in the way. But when it did happen; I always heard the expression, "wearing a boy on a wrist." I think at that moment is the first time I ever felt it. When it was over with, we both got connected and we've stayed very good friends, and still get together every once in a while. But that one time was just special, it was just a memorable moment for me.

I mean, at first he didn't think he was going to do it. There's lots of guys who you can just literally slide your hand into their asses. To me, they're not even worth doing this with. This guy wanted it to happen, but he was afraid to, and it was working with him...that he trusted me long enough to allow it to. Just that he trusted me. When it happened, we were together the whole night afterwards, just holding each other. I have to admit, it was probably the top sexual experience of my life.

John

Fisting is very sexual. Once we were team fisting one guy. There were four of us taking turns and it took about an hour. Everybody got their turn and everybody got off. We convinced him to get into this, because we knew that he likes it.

Did I get off? Of course I did. Twice.

Mark Frazier

As a top, it would probably be the raw emotion of playing with somebody and touching their inner soul, because I think that when a bottom allows you to have their trust; you can actually feel the person's heartbeat that you've been playing with. Because you're so in tune with the person. And then, if the bottom allows himself to let go of all the trust and transfer that all to you, saying that you are in control, you'll be able to have just as many endorphin rushes as the bottom.

To me, the ability to give up trust, the ability to say I am not in control any longer, and allow that top to take control of my body for their pleasure and also, for lack of a better term, to be able to expand my horizons…and my ass.

The very first time I was fisted, it was somebody I had known, somebody who I had a friendship with, somebody I had played with before as a top and as a bottom. Knowing, going into the scene, that it was going to be something I had never done before, relinquishing control to the top, and allowing myself to totally enjoy a scene that I had only read about, thought about, had never participated in. Then being able to open up and take something up my ass larger than I have every taken in my life. When we first started with the fingers, actually with the Crisco, the first thing I kept saying is, *I can't do it, I can't do it, I can't do it, I can't do it.* Through his voice, through his coaxing me into it, knowing that it was something I wanted, then finding a way that I could give up that trust, that was the hardest part. But once I gave up the trust, I knew that I could trust this person completely and I could give up control. I can compare the first time that I was fisted to breath control, because you cannot enjoy a scene in breath control play without trusting the person you're playing with. The same thing happens in a fisting scene. If you don't trust the person you're playing with, either as a top or a bottom, you're not going to enjoy the scene. If you can relinquish control and trust the person you're playing with, it's going to allow you to achieve probably one of the most spectacular feelings that a person can experience.

Master Warren

It's a sense of power, control, and trust. I think those are the three elements that do it for me as a top, which is the only way I do it. When you reach up inside and you feel someone's heart beating almost in your hands, it gives you a great sense of power. Through that power is the sense of trust that the boy is giving you by letting you reach inside him.

I have two favorite moments. When I was basically little more than a kid still in college, I went to Mexico. I picked up a beach boy on the beach and I didn't know the slightest thing about BDSM, or leather, or anything at that time, took him back to my room and began playing with him, and before I knew it I had my fist up his ass. And I didn't even realize what happened, except I knew that it drove him crazy with pleasure. So that was my very first fisting experience before I even knew what to call it or that there even was such a thing!

On a subsequent trip, after I got out of college, back to New York City, I was wearing my Future Farmers of America T-shirt, FFA, and somebody in a bar commented, "FFA? FFA? We can't even get a barful here…they had a national convention in Kansas City, and we didn't know about it?" On that trip, I met a guy who lived down in the Village and spent quite a bit of time with him, and he was really, really heavy into fisting. I was still a neophyte, didn't know anything about it, and I remember fisting him for hours. It was such a new experience for me, and I really was thrilled by it. I remember one of the things I had never experienced before was lying on the bed with my arm up and him squatting over my fist. He would get up and go to work in the morning, and I'd have to fist him before he went to work, and as soon as he got home I'd be fisting him and using different play toys and stuff. Those were probably my most memorable when I think of my fisting experiences.

Master Z

My most memorable experience was going to a gay bar in Dallas-Fort Worth when I was down there for some training, and I was watching a fisting video in the back room of a bar. I don't even remember what the name of the bar was! This gentleman came over to me and he saw my red handkerchief in my back pocket. He said, "I really like your handkerchief and I *really* like your forearms." I looked at him and when I turned back to the screen, I realized it was the guy on the video! It was the first time that I got both arms into somebody. Well, when I was double fisting, the interesting part was I could take my fingers, turn my hand and turn my fingers, and I could see my fingers outside of there, it was just very, very hollow. After I got done he turned around and he said to me, "okay now fuck me," and I said, "you've got to be kidding. With what?!?" That turned into a very, very hot, hot scene. The first time that I got both arms into somebody and it was memorable.

Richard

As a bottom, for years I've always had the fantasy of having my ass played with, but I never did anything. And then after I got fucked a few times, I started playing with toys and somehow I was on a site and I seen this fisting thing. I didn't know what it was, I never knew people did that. And then I came down to one of Ed's gatherings, he had Fisting 101. I came down and watched that and I guess the next fisting party he had I came down and I got fisted and I enjoyed it. I've probably been fisted now maybe 8 times, 9 times, and in between I play with my toys. I have some big toys that I play with. The feeling of being filled up makes me feel good.

I guess I would have to say, actually, the first one. When he kept saying, "we're close, we're close," and then all of a sudden he didn't say anything. I knew it was in and I had that feeling and it felt very good.

Master Jazz (a cautionary tale)

I would imagine that for each person it's quite different, but then again it could be the same. Of course, the fistee is receiving more of the pleasure than the fister, in that respect. And a fistee once asked me himself, what do I get out of it? I, personally, get out of it pleasure from his pleasure, watching him go through all these different emotions, having his body go through these different orgasms, as you go forward, deeper or harder, depending on the individual themselves. It is an art form, it's a science, a science of your anatomy — if you don't know what you're doing, don't do it, because you literally have someone's life in your hands, if you pardon the pun. It's an extreme fetish in one respect, as it's not an easy one to get into even though so many people think it is. It's an enjoyment, again, because as a top, as a master, as a daddy, I'm giving the bottom, the slave, the boy, the more enjoyment of it, and then again maybe getting it more so, because I'm the one who's doing it to them. So it's a real two-way street, though it may seem more one-way than the other at times. That's more my enjoyment out of it.

My most memorable fisting session? That's a good one. I've really had many. I've been told that a lot of guys cannot handle my mitts, as I like to call them, and of course one has to realize that whichever one is your dominant writing hand is, of course, the larger hand. So a lot of times you may have to settle for the lesser one, or the smaller hand. Of course if you're right-handed, that's the larger hand, even though it doesn't seem as much, but it is.

The one scene that I recount constantly is with one particular gentleman who, unfortunately, is no longer with us, may he rest in peace. We shoved in him colored Crisco balls and metal eggs, and that was a major commotion. He cursed us all out after he was done being fisted and kept passing these slime shits all over the floor in color, not realizing what the hell was going on, and someone had to follow him with a squeegee. After that point, he took a breather, and again we started with the metal eggs. In those days, we were so literally twisted to the tits, we forgot how many eggs we put in him and we left one in him when we went to sleep. We woke up the following morning and he had, I wouldn't say excruciating, but really, he had the feeling of having to relieve himself. When he thusly went to the lavatory, the next thing you heard was plop, crash, bam, splash. Because of the pressure his body had built up, it forced the egg out of him and broke the commode literally in half. It was like a clean cut. He was still sitting there with a waterspout going up his ass, giving him a douche at the same time! This man stood soaking wet at maybe 110 pounds if anything, and was a medium size drink of water, but with this insatiable hole that just could not get enough. Not many people can realize what I'm saying here, but of course if you were there like I was, seeing the visualization of this is a whole 'nother story.

Gary

Well, I've always sort of been into ass play. I like to totally be able to relax and let go. My nickname is the Zen Master, because I don't find it necessary to use poppers. I can just relax and get right into it, it's just a sort of self-control. I like to top, but I'm very 50-50. So it goes both ways.

Memorable? Oh, yeah, a real good one. A friend came up for a couple of days from down South. We were messing around and he finally managed to take my fist. So he's on a bed and the next thing he says is, "I want to stand up." So we maneuvered around and I'm sitting on the floor with my hand Statue of Liberty style! Do you know how much leverage your ass has when you're standing? We're in this battle of wills, you know, because I thought, if I relax even a little bit, it's going to break my wrist. So we're having this battle of wills, and the next thing I knew he just shoots all over me. It was like, wow, and then there was real leverage. He just about crushed my hand, and it was a really, really hot scene. We both put it on our top ten.

Mr. Bratman

I can answer your questions. The first would be that your power and control feels very complete when you have a boy bound in a sling and your fist up his ass. As for the most memorable, it was when a boy came twice while I was fisting him, without any other stimulation. He was an Australian coming through San Francisco on a 'round-the-world ticket and wanted a 48-hour scene. I had the sling up and decided to fist him, even though we hadn't really talked about it beforehand. When I later talked to him on line, he told me he'd been fisted a couple of times before. I don't usually do a recap with boys while they are here, and I should warn you...I have big hands!

Master Lance

Fisting gives me great pleasure. I was at the Mineshaft fisting some unknown person while I was getting my cock sucked and ass eaten. I was fisting someone and a guy came over and started to suck my cock, and then someone came over and started to eat my ass. When you initiated a scene in a place like that, everyone wanted to be a part of it.

Ron

What draws me is the intimacy between two people. Because it's very much about trust. I'm going to trust that whoever's on top is going to be listening to what I say and getting more intimate that way.

Just about every one is memorable, if you really want to know. But the first time you actually take a fist is probably the most memorable, and who it was. I mean, the first time you actually succeed in taking a fist. Fisting isn't something that you just simply say "I'm going to do this today." It just doesn't happen that way, and you succeed or, well, most of the fisting is getting there. Getting onto the wrist is just the success of it.

Jody (Bearcumco)

I met an amazing man when I was traveling for a living. I was in Western Massachusetts and he was in Boston doing the exact same job I did, and he was a fisting bottom mostly, but versatile. We hit it off and started dating, and after about three months of working my butt, he finally slid in, and it was amazing. Then I moved to Reno with the boy I was dating and living with; when I finally was able to put my extra-large hand in his hole, he cried like a child who got his best Christmas present. With the boy in Reno, he trusted me to tie him down and talk him into relaxing and trusting me to use his most sacred place with something that was not supposed to normally be there. That was probably the most memorable, because we shared a love that was so intense, and his finally being able to do that for Daddy made the most intense connection we would ever have.

John

My partner was into it, but I was always kind of *"Eww!* Why would you want to do *that?"* Then one night I was in a bookstore in San Diego. Just there to cruise and suck dick. A gentleman in full leather was there and wanted me to play with his ass. So I played a little here and played a little there, with no lube other than what was in his ass already. Then slowly it was two fingers, then three, then four; then suddenly it was my whole fist up there. After that, I was hooked. I thought to myself; let me see if I can try to do that. I started out small, and worked my way up to dildos. I really didn't get into fisting till I moved from the west coast to the east coast. It just kind of happened. I like the width aspect, the bigness, and the fullness. I'm not a big depth person, I enjoy the in and out. I guess being fucked is a really big aspect of it. I don't play with toys very much anymore; it's got to be a hand now.

My first time taking was at FFA in DC, and I'm thinking, oh God, this is really good. That first time, when the top's hand kind of goes in and you're going

"Aughh! Take it out!" Then, for the second time, you just want to relax and get to experience this. So I went back for a second round, and as I'm relaxing into it, the host of the party screams. "They're towing cars! You're parked at the gas station!" I was out of that sling in four seconds, downstairs and dressed. My, and one other person's, car was still there.

Red Bear Mike, VA

For me, the biggest thing that gets me off is their pleasure. Whether that pleasure is the pain aspect of it or the pleasure part, it's the response of their body and mind. That's where the excitement of fisting comes from.

The most exciting scene I had involved fisting, but ended with a fire extinguisher. He was tied face down with his ass propped up. I opened him up with toys and then with my hands, and I'd brought a commercial fire extinguisher. Not the really huge one, but not the little home one that you keep under the sink. The commercial one for the home that's a bit bigger. In the course of that evening, we used a 40-ounce beer bottle, my hands and we finished with the fire extinguisher. This was someone I'd regularly played with, and I was moving, so this was to be our last play session together. He'd always wanted to take both my hands, but he's a relatively small guy, and I have pretty large hands. So even though we'd played for years, it just didn't seem physically possible, short of sending him to the emergency room. He would leave the door unlocked and I would come in and assault him. That was the fantasy. He wasn't aware of what it was till after it was in, because I had him blindfolded. I was also using a gas mask with poppers on him. Once it was in, I released him so he could feel it. I knew, for him, he got off very much on reaching back and feeling my arm or forearm and seeing how deep I was in him. He then reached back and realized it was a fire extinguisher, and that made him cum.

He's one of the few people that I have fisted to the extreme that we'd have to tie his dick up, or he'll cum before he's ready, much less before I'm ready for him to cum. He was always a very fun partner from that standpoint, because a lot of fisting bottoms tend to lose their erections. It's just overstimulation. It's not that they're not into the scene, but that their prostate is so stimulated that their dick will go soft. It isn't like when you're fucking, and you can always reach around and feel a hard dick and know that they're having a good time. You have to connect on a different level. But he's one of those rare people that, no matter what you do to his ass, his dick is always hard. The slightest manipulation to one side, and he'll shoot, even if he's not touching himself. But like a lot of people, once he's cum, the party's over. When he'd start to orgasm, I'd need to pull out, because afterwards it was much more of a chore to get out. He'd be too sensitive.

Generally, I can't get my hands into a newbie. Usually only four fingers or so is all they can handle before they've cum or they're getting sore. I'm not a good starter person. So this man was a very experienced fisting bottom to start with, before this last game.

Jim "Gagbear" Grrowl

There's only one thing more exciting than hearing a boy moan and groan while I work my fist up his hole, and that's to hear the same moans and groans muffled by a thick gag stuffed in his mouth. A ripe jock strap, a dirty bandanna, a few strips of duct tape or a big rubber ball: they're all good to mute the erotic cries of a helpless slave as I slowly open him up. *MMMmmmppppffff!!*

Michael

Fisting is a new experience for me; I have not taken a full fist yet. I'm working up to it. I'm going through a transition in my life, because of my age. I'm no longer topping, and I'm moving towards becoming a fisting bottom. My partner is very skilled as a fisting top, and I was watching him enjoy other men, so I thought I'd try to expand the horizons for myself.

Topbinder

Although there had been one or two attempts at fisting prior to this major experience, this one was an evening at the baths. Those days when rampant experimentation and sex took place without latex, and before we knew of anything coming down the road to change our habits. I was living in San Francisco at the time, and went to my favorite haunt for the sexual smorgasbord, the Ritch Street Baths.

One open door kept catching my eye. Inside was one pleasant looking man, poised in dog style on his cot, his face towards the wall. What was signaled as I walked by each time was an ass desiring to be serviced, nothing more, nothing less. Walking in the semi-dark, draped in a towel, my mind drifted to prior experiences that left me wanting an experienced ass to explore, rather than the novice participants of the past.

I entered the room, leaving the door open as I reached with my left hand to caress his ass cheeks and glide my fingers to his fuck hole. There was a slight moan as I placed my fingers on his tight lips. I retracted and spit on my fingers, returning to his hole to slide a digit in. This brought an even stronger moan and a soft uttering of "please, Sir."

By now, my cock was fully alive and my balls were beginning to strain. I shut the door and went behind him, on my knees, and reached for the lube on his shelf. A hit of poppers, a load of lube on my hand, and I began to slowly slide in and out of his ass, one finger, then two, three, and with four his moans began to deepen from the deep well of desire that an animal in heat would moan.

I prepared my hand with more lube, and folded my thumb to narrow my hand and provide a smoother entry. A rhythmic pressure, in and out, slowly opened his ass for my whole hand. As it slid into his waiting ass, he growled at me. "Sir, thank you for taking my ass." No more verbal responses would follow, instead, rhythmic moans of animal pleasure as I moved in and out, then deeper into his ass.

His ass was warm, moist, and soft as velvet as it was entered and explored. Resting against my palm, I could feel the pulsations of his heart through his artery, a pounding gauge to tell me his excitement without speaking a word. As I would glide forward, his hips would move towards me in acceptance. A ritual of movement, synchronized by his heartbeat, encased in warm velvet. I now entered his ass so I could piston pump my cock within him. His hips moved in synchronized motion to the thrusts of my hips, burying my cock into my own hand, inside his ass. With my free hand, I brought the poppers to his nose and then to mine. That done, I moved my lubed hand to his throbbing cock, working it in motion with our bodies. This surreal entry into the passion that builds under my influence was heightened by his deepening moans, the increased movement of his hips, and his begging again for me, "deeper, Sir."

My rhythm increased to match his own, with that pulsating hole. Deeper until my balls were ready to scream, and he arched his back with a deep guttural shout as he shot his cum into my hand and on the cot. Unable and unwilling to stop, I shot hot loads inside into my own hand and his ass. And then, as if every motion was planned, he slowly retreated on his belly to the cot. The pulsing heartbeat was slowing as I first retracted my cock from his ass. Then a slow exit of my wrist, then my hand. He was breathing steadily, softly. Then he turned to face me for the first time, saying "Thank you Sir, thank you for giving me what I wanted."

I reached down, grabbed him by the front of his neck and nuzzled into the back of his neck with my mouth. "No, thank you for making me so welcome," I replied. I draped my towel around my waist, and quietly left the room as he drifted off to sleep. Looking back, as I shut the door, I knew this would be one experience that would remain in my memories.

To The Elbows

I had my very first FF experience back in 1979 at the then infamous Mineshaft in NYC's Greenwich Village. I was with a couple of friends who introduced me to this after-hours orgy place, complete with slings, chains, toilets for water sports, bathtubs, etc. I got high on some LSD that night and was taken by a hot guy to a room with some slings. This guy put me in the sling, tied me up in it spread-eagle and proceeded to Crisco my hole and have me use poppers. Next thing I knew, the guy got in me to his wrist and fucked my hole with it, eventually pistoning in and out. To me, when I came down from my high, it was a great experience, since I never thought that arm fucking was possible. I sure knew better after that time! Anyways, over the years, I have gotten more into FF and getting fisted. I have, for the past three years, learned to get elbow fucked since I developed a lot more confidence between myself and my partner, whom I am together with over 15 years. Getting fisted is a mind blowing and awesome experience, but one has to be really wanting and ready for it. It is definitely not for everyone. I'm trying to, and with the help of some party favors, get a foot up my hole. I've made it to the ankle so far.

Daddy Bill

As you may already know, I began fisting guys when I was in my mid-twenties and now I'll be 68 in January. That's a lot of fisting! I've fisted both experienced bottoms and properly opened many newbies. My buddy, John, whom you met at IML with me, was a virgin when he met me a couple of years ago.

I could certainly tell you of my experiences over more than four decades of topping. You probably can guess that absolutely no one, even in the ordinary gay community, ever spoke about fisting forty years ago. It was very much a secret and completely underground practice. There was no such thing as walking into a leather shop and seeing a sling on display that could be purchased! My first sling, which still hangs on the wall of my dungeon in a place of honor, was hand-made for me by an older buddy who happened to be a leather craftsman and who actually mentored me as a young top in my twenties. Incidentally, about a year ago, I sent my original sling to Patrick Brumm in Ft. Lauderdale to make a pattern of its unique design. He made me duplicates with new leather for me and a friend, and is also offering them for sale on his website.

By the way, I'll be having a long and intense fisting session tomorrow. By long, I mean many hours and by intense, I mean it will include restraints, CBT, TT, hoods, gags, and various other devices of pain and pleasure. Many men are into fisting but not real leathersex; I'm into the entire package of submission and fisting. I did not expound on the spiritual and transcendent aspects of fisting, both of which are absolutely essential to me as a top. In fact, I often use the "altar metaphor," the sling being an altar upon which a male surrenders himself and his masculine energy in communion with another male. When total surrender in bondage is included, the sacrifice and surrender are complete. You can well imagine that what I seek cannot be comprehended nor achieved at the popular fisting play parties, and that is why they don't entice me in the least.

Actually, I was invited to attend a fist party during IML in 2004 and, although I enjoyed meeting and chatting with several men, I fisted not a single one the entire evening. The scene of rows of symmetrically-aligned slings occupied by bottoms, artificially hungry for a fist because of Crystal Meth ingestion, struck me as immensely sad.

BK Bear Maxx

For a number of years, Maxx wrote for Drummer Magazine under his pen-name, Michael Agreve. He also contributed stories to Bear Magazine and Bulk Male. Recently, he contributed a nonfiction article to a Lambda Award-winning book that dealt with sexuality and gay disabled men. Currently, he writes an advice column for Bent Voices, an on-line magazine for gay, disabled men. He is currently completing a fiction novel and continues to explore the world of kinky sex, both recreationally and for additional material for his writing.

I've been into fisting since the days of the Mineshaft. I'd figure around 1976 or '77, when I had a loft off Canal St. I was seeing people at the Mineshaft that were into it, people that were getting it. Keep in mind that I've always liked any kind of kink, so that had a great appeal. I've never been into actual fucking, either getting or giving. With fisting, then, you have a greater control over the person. It was also one of those things that I love, in that fisting is very cerebral, very mental, as well as very physical. You have to control your mind in order to control your hand. You can give the person involved pleasure and a lot of pain. To me, I love the combination of the pain and pleasure, especially if they're done at the same time. You can turn the pain into the pleasure very easily, once the person is relaxed. You can add another layer on it, which a lot of fisters don't, but I like to. You can suck on the person while they are being fisted, you can work on their feet, which I like doing when I'm fisting somebody. Sucking on the feet, licking the feet, because I've always been into feet. There you have somebody's feet, if they're in a sling, right at your shoulder level or right at your face level. It almost seemed to me to be an automatic add-on, that a person would be exposed that way. You have the feet, which can be easily manipulated, and the same thing with a person's cock. You're adding additional layers onto it, along with the basic kink of the fisting. But you can really make it a lot more than simply that.

The first man I ever fisted was at the Mineshaft. There was somebody that was in one of the slings being fisted, and I was watching. I hung around and after the guy who was working on him was finished, he asked me if I wanted to try it. Which I did, and the minute I got into it, I knew I had a good feel for it. I was able to gauge by the person's face and the noises he'd make, if it was pleasurable or a little too painful.

Now that places like the Mineshaft are pretty much gone, sometimes you'll find there are people who need to be mentored into fisting. There was one person that I worked with who was very new to it. This man had cerebral palsy and I'd met him when we did a group scene at a friend's house. The owner of the house was very into fisting and is also a multiple-disabled person. We had played at one point, and later found out this new man was just getting into fisting. It was the three of us later, his friend, him and myself. We did some other play, but primarily focused on fisting. I did actually get to fist him and was one of his very first. What I tried with him was also explain what he needed to do to prepare himself as a fisting bottom. You know, the physical stuff, the enemas, douching, but also preparing himself mentally.

Because, for me, fisting has never been the one and only thing, just like bondage isn't the one and only thing. I like all of it as part of a scene, but we did other things that led up to the fisting. The fisting was sort of the finale to the whole thing. I realized that once the fisting occurred, he'd probably cum, but not be physically able to do much more, as he'd be exhausted. He was one of the first that I probably really mentored. Most of the men I've encountered are pretty much into it, so they didn't need much training. A lot of times now on-line I run into guys who say I really want to try it, get into fisting, so what I'll do is drop them hints. I'll tell them to work butt plugs in, to use graduating dildos, different sizes, to stretch themselves out. I can help them along that way, even if we never get to meet.

Still, most of the fisting scenes I've gotten into have been with people that are pretty much into it. They knew how to take it; they knew what they had to do. They would come prepared. They'd have their can of Crisco waiting in the room so you would know what they were into. I went to the Barracks Bathhouse a couple of times when spending three weeks in Toronto. It seemed like everybody there was into fisting; the one night I was literally able to go from one room to the next, fisting one guy after another, after another. That was just astounding. It was the most amazing sexual time I've ever had.

I'm a pretty big guy. I am not beginner's hands. There was one guy I met up with about two months ago. He could barely take it. Once we had finished, he was so exhausted that I figured he probably wouldn't want a rematch. Surprisingly, he has contacted me since. For somebody starting out, they'll probably want a small fist, but for somebody well experienced, they can probably take my big one. Amazingly, there was one guy at The Barracks who was very short. I mean maybe five feet, five-one. He was taking one of those monster dildos that had to be six to eight inches wide. We played a bit and I did fist him, and surprisingly, he could take that dildo incredibly well, but a fist was a lot harder. Especially my fist, because it is big. There was another guy there who was very tall, and he took the fist all the way up to my elbow in one thrust. To him it was like the easiest thing in the world. Everybody was talking about it. Yes, an extremely well-trained butt. He was very tall, I don't know if that had anything to do with it. But everyone who fisted him got way up to the elbow. With other bottoms, you have to work it more.

The work is one of the things that attracts me to fisting, it's extremely intimate. You're literally inside another person. To me it's a night and day difference, when you're inside with your cock. Most people see this as the ultimate intimacy, but when you're inside with your hand, you can feel the person's heartbeat. You know that you're as deep inside a human being as you can go. I think part of it is the mental kick, that here's somebody who is doing something that very few men can achieve. To take a big hand, to love it that way, it's a total mental kick combined with the physical part. That you're doing something that most people would look on as totally sick and maybe deranged for wanting it. People may ask why somebody would want that pain; but again, it's pain that turns to pleasure. There's no other physical activity that can, in my estimation, give you that kind of mental and physical level of, not just power, but achievement on the bottom's part. Even of a certain intimacy, I mean, once you've had your hand up somebody, you can't get more intimate.

There's certainly an element where each part becomes stronger. For myself, my take on a lot of the dominance/submission, top/bottom thing, I have a very different dynamic than a lot of people out there. First of all, to me, the bottom is not an object. If you're going to do something that has the great potential to hurt him, as fisting certainly does, you've got to respect that person a lot. You have to look at them as somebody who will feel pain, who could be torn up inside if you're not careful. There's also the level of control; you can look at him as a piece of dirt, because he's bottom submissive, or you could take the mind of that person to different levels of experience. For a lot of fisting bottoms, they don't get men who will lick or touch them, there's just the heavy thrusting. I think if you give that other level to a bottom, also showing that you have a certain caring for him even as you're controlling him, you'll come away with a mental scene with the physical just coming together in a very different way. It's more that just getting in, getting out and getting off.

I am personally attracted to men with disabilities and features that others may not like, like guys with very small cocks. I think they tend to compensate for not having what they think most people want between their legs by having that between their ass. The most profound scenes and experiences I've had have been the ones I've had with men with disabilities. You're adding another layer to it; you're dealing with men who are usually rejected simply because of their physical looks. Sometimes you have to adjust a bit more because there might be other physical ramifications because of the way their bodies are shaped or the way they work. But I think giving pleasure to somebody who is usually overlooked is very profound.

It gives me a lot more of that mental kick. I always thought the ideal person into fisting would be a double leg amputee, where you have no legs to interfere with total access to the asshole. I've spoken to other guys that have the same interest. In the world of gay sex, a lot of this becomes extremely political. The notion of, do I want the most beautiful body to fist? Especially if you're at a fisting party, or a scene like The Mineshaft, where everything is visible and people see what you're doing. To me, to find someone who is not only kinky and into real unusual and out-there play, but also who doesn't fit the stereotype. Maybe somebody who looks like a milquetoast or a very nerdy guy, but will open his ass to you incredibly. The first guy I ever fisted was like that. He wasn't a stud by any means. It was one of the reasons I liked the fact that he was there with his open ass, and it was as good as fisting some big muscle ass.

SEVEN: RAISE YOUR HAND IF YOU'RE SURE

By Michael Agreve

"Darren, how long are you going to be in there? There are others in this house, you know."

He heard his mother's nagging voice through the bathroom door.

"Just a minute, Mom, I'll be right out," he said. But he knew better. He looked down at the open magazine, his bright blue eyes scanning every inch of the body on the printed page. It was as perfect a body as anyone could want to hope for, with its thick musculature, no doubt steroid assisted, and the huge swollen cock that sported a gob of clear precum picking up the light from the photographer's reflected bulb. He reached with his left hand for his own dick; almost as sizable as the one in the porno magazine, but so far unexposed to anyone else who might be impressed by its length and thickness and equally impressive expanse of dangling nut sac.

"Darren, stop being so selfish. I swear, the older you get the more you think only about yourself. If your father was here...."

But his father wasn't there. And he knew that as much as his mother bellowed and bullied, she would always remember just who and what Darren was and slink back, apologetic and guilty in equal doses. It was a mental quirk he loved taking full advantage of. He knew that if he chose to, he would be free to sit there as long as he wanted, jerking on his stiff prick while he searched for the one photo that would finally get his man juice pushed out through his covered cock hole. He knew that he probably shouldn't be dropping a load so soon before he would be leaving. But he knew that if he didn't, his boner would sprout up at the most inopportune time, like during the long bus ride, where some stranger might spot it and decide that it was some sort of snake that had to be clobbered to death before it bit the man in whose pants it resided. Still, there might be someone else on the bus who might see it for what it was and decide that it needed to be treated a lot more gently. That would certainly give his mother pause, at least pause in the long list of instructions and warnings he would get from her the minute he headed close to the front door.

"First of all, Darren, I don't think I have to remind you never to speak to strangers," he could almost hear his mother saying. "You don't know who you might find on that bus. Nice people don't go running off for weekends with strangers you never even met, while I have to stay here all by myself wondering if someone has a knife to your throat or worse." He had no idea what could possibly be worse than a knife to his throat, unless it was one more weekend spent in the tiny house he shared with his mother in Plattsburgh, New York, which was about as far away from anything as imaginable, including something that remotely resembled a sex life for him. It was that lack of a sex life which forced him to sit in the upstairs bathroom, working on his sizable prick, while he imagined just what he would do with any number of the men whose crotches were spread across the glossy magazine that he tucked into his pants as he left the bathroom and hurried down the staircase to where his suitcases lay. He had decided at the last minute that he would take the magazine with him, just in case he needed it for some pod-pulling inspiration.

"Well, look who's made an appearance," his mother said, unaware that he had just finished dropping a load. "Look at you, Darren, you look all flushed," she added, unaware that he had just finished flushing a couple million of his prize sperm cells down the toilet along with the tissue he had used to wipe them off his chest.

There was a lot that Darren could have said at that moment by way of a response. Instead, he just smiled back at her, aware that he could always melt her reserve with one well-placed grin. "You know I hate to nag, Darren, but are you sure you want to go to that retreat or whatever they call it? What do they have there out in the woods that you don't have here?"

"A nagging pain in the ass mother who still thinks I'm twelve years old," he wanted to respond. Instead, he walked over to her and put his hand on her shoulder, aware that it was concern for his well-being, not just irrational anxiety that motivated her to speak....and speak....and speak. "I'll be all right, Mom. I'm thirty-one years old. I'm not a baby any more. I work, I have a social life....well, sort of. I can take care of myself, Mom....honest."

He knew that nothing he could say would stop her from conjuring up scenarios of kidnap and rape, to say nothing of indoctrination by what she believed was a group arranging a spiritual retreat at a campsite in the wilds of Finger Lakes. Well, it was a spiritual retreat of sorts. But not the kind she imagined it would be.

"I worry about you, Darren. Ever since you got that computer and started talking to people on the Internet, well, you've changed. You're not the same boy I know and love."

She was right. He was not the same as when he had first gotten the computer and discovered that if he couldn't have something resembling a sex life first hand, a sex life on line was a good close second. And while he could no longer be called a boy chronologically, he had found many men out there who wanted to consider him one, although not on the same level that his mother could ever imagine.

"So, you have everything packed?" she added, more or less resigned to his leaving for the weekend.

"I do, Mom," he said. "Everything I need."

It was not a lie. It just wasn't the entire truth. What his suitcase contained was all the expected items: clean underwear, a couple of pairs of socks, insect repellant, a tooth brush and toothpaste, one pair of long pants and two pairs of shorts, a couple of shirts, and three butt plugs of varying sizes plus a collection of dildos that ranged from six inches to one that resembled no human cock he had ever seen in print or on line. Oh yes, and lubricant....lots of lubricant.

"Don't worry, Mom. I'll be all right. I've known Sam for three years now. He's a cool guy."

Cool, of course, was not exactly how most people would describe Sam. When he had first e-mailed his picture to him, Darren had been amazed that a man who looked as hot as Sam had sent him an instant message in a chat room. When they started talking, the heat had only increased, making Darren realize that there were many other men out there who seemed anxious to make their butt holes the center of not just their universe, but the entire galaxy for anyone who wanted to hitchhike onto it. For Darren, that encounter had been the first "opening" into the world of anal kink that would now culminate with his spending a hotly anticipated long holiday weekend with other men with the same interest. But excitement carried with it an equal amount of uncertainty for Darren. Sure, Sam had liked what he had seen in the photo that he had sent back, with the image of his mother standing next to him digitally cropped. But Sam wasn't like most men out there in cyber-land. For one, Sam was switchable and could take as good as he gave. And he had seen in Darren something he had seen in few others who had responded to his innocuous "Hey guy" on an instant pop-up. Sam saw in Darren the possibility for added layers of kink. But would others see it as well?

"Well, I just wish there was a way I could contact you there, Darren. You know, you could get a cell phone like I suggested. Personally, I would not want to go to a place where there were no phone hooks-ups. What if there's a fire in the woods? You know how hot and dry it's been lately. What if some wild animal attacks?"

"There's a reason why it's called a 'retreat,' Mom. You're supposed be able to enjoy nature and discover your own inner peace. No televisions, no computers, and outside contacts, especially calls. And they have phones for emergencies. It's not like I'm going off to Borneo or something like that. It's Lake Cayuga. Somehow, I don't think there are many wolves and wild boars left there. And speaking of going, I'd better get a move on. The taxi should be here any minute."

He stared into his mother's unconvinced face. It wasn't exactly that he was ashamed of being gay and couldn't tell her where he was really going because of that. She had suspected as much about him when he had entered his late teens with no dates looming, let alone any marriage prospects now that he had entered his thirties. But how do you tell a mother that what you want from a male partner was not the expected suck and fuck, but to also have your butt hole impaled onto whatever part of the man's hand that your slowly expanded hole could take? It was why he had opened up a Post Office box in town to receive the steady supply of anal toys he had acquired in the past few years. It was also why he had finally put his foot down and told his mother in no uncertain terms that a locked room door meant that his need for privacy had to be respected and that once in there only a knock could gain someone other than himself entry. She had respected that, aware that she too had some needs for privacy, however limited. So he had placed his growing collection of toys in his closet, aware that she would not venture there for fear that his anger at her intrusion might bring about his leaving the house they had shared since his father had died nine years ago. Still, he was glad that the collection was now in his suitcase and not still in the closet, which she might be tempted to rummage through in his absence.

"Well then, Darren, I guess that all I can say is have a good time. Be safe. And remember, if you should happen to be near a phone, you can always call home collect. A call just to let me know that you arrived in one piece wouldn't hurt, would it?"

He tried not to laugh. He knew that sooner or later he would have to make decisions about whether or not he wanted to continue to live his life mixed up so closely with hers or seek the kind of independence Sam had been encouraging him to gain. They had talked about it more and more lately, with Sam encouraging him to think about trying to get a place of his own, a place where he could have some freedom and peace of mind, to say nothing of the kind of sex life Darren sorely wanted.

"Boy," Sam had said to him during their first phone conversation, months after they had talked on line, "you'll never become the person you need to be tied to the old lady's apron strings." Of course, Darren had never mentioned that potentially spending his life as someone else's "boy," even if it was Sam himself, might not be much of a change, except for the possibilities of endless sex. Darren knew enough about his needs to know that he enjoyed giving up control to someone else, especially someone older and more authoritative than himself, like Sam. From the onset of their friendship, Darren had known that Sam expected certain levels of obedience form him, levels that he was more than prepared to furnish. But he also knew that he was far too new to being exposed to the dynamic of dominance and submission to say that it was something that he was prepared to do 24/7. Their weekend together would at least give Darren a chance to explore the chemistry between the two of them and to see if Sam would bring out that part of Darren that knew that what the other man wanted from him sexually was far more important than what he thought he wanted from the same man. Darren also knew that fully testing the dynamic between the two of them would not be played out during their time together in privacy or even in the dungeon setting that Sam had created in his own home just outside of Rochester. Darren would have to make his debut into the world of kink that he yearned to be a part of in the presence of others, many others, with many eyes on him as Sam guided him to where his mind and body knew it needed to be heading.

"Think of it as fisting boot camp," Sam had said when he had first told Darren about the upcoming annual event. "There'll be plenty of guys like you there, guys who have never actually taken a fist, but who need to know if it's something they want to commit their man-holes to. And there'll be lots of guys like me…well, not exactly like me. You could say I'm kind of unique in the fisting scenes in more ways than one. Most men you meet there are either Top or bottom or at least versatile in some things. Me, I like it all, although I've got to say, there's nothing like controlling a man from the inside out. Just think about it, boy. You can watch others being pigs. You can be a fucking pig yourself. You can also watch me giving and taking fists and dicks and piss and loving every minute. And maybe, if you're lucky, we can find a guy to do the two of us at the same time. Wouldn't be a first for me, boy. So think about it, boy. I'm willing to pick you up at your place if that's what you want. You can also take the bus most of the way and I can meet you. Whichever way, boy, I would be real proud to have you there sharing my bed."

Darren did think about it. He thought about the long hours he had spent in his room with an oversized dildo up his rectum while he watched guys on DVD's taking full hands from equally muscled studs who might turn the tables and claim some fists up their expansive holes, just like Sam had told him he liked to do. He had dropped endless loads onto his chest, the smell of his freshly spilled spunk driving him to reload a DVD to get to the part that would help him cap it off with another semen cocktail that he could later suck out from his ripened jock strap. But as much as he enjoyed those long sessions with himself and his dick and his asshole, it could not compare to having someone else share the kink with him. He knew that sooner or later fantasy alone would not serve in lieu of the full-fledged sex life that he knew so many men out there enjoyed. He knew that no rubber cock up his ass or porno image on the screen could replace the one-on-one that was needed to make a fisting scene come alive in a man's mind and in his butt hole. As good as their on-line and phone conversations had been, which was incredibly good by any standards, Darren knew that it needed to be a lot better and that the only thing that could make it better was to do it in person, which was why he had finally agreed to fill out the application for the Labor Day Pig-Out sponsored by the national fisting group that Sam had been a member of for the past fifteen years.

Once at the bus station, Darren was convinced that he had made the right move. No matter how much trepidation and downright uncertainty he felt, which he admitted to himself was a lot, he never lost sight of the fact that he was traveling towards what could very well be the start of his belated sex life. Even as the bus made its way towards the small-town stop where Sam would pick Darren up for the final few miles to the campsite, Darren's mind stayed focused on the feel of the butt plug that Sam had ordered him to come with deep inside his well-greased fuck hole. It was the one sensation that egged him on even when part of his brain told him that he might be fooling himself for thinking that others would accept him as part of their already established world of kink. He felt the almost treasuring searing of that plug deep inside him as he stood up and retrieved his overhead luggage before departing from the bus. He wondered if everyone staring at him as he left knew exactly why he seemed to walk so slowly and deliberately, or if it was because of the usual reason he was getting so many unwanted looks. But once he saw Sam's pickup truck parked in the lot next to the bus station, Darren stopped wondering about the other passengers as his mind latched on to another kind of insecure train of thought. Even at a distance it was obvious that the man sitting in the cab of the truck was as hot a piece of ass as any that could be found. Would Darren be remotely the kind of man he could see himself spending time with in the company of others who might judge or question his attraction to the thirty year-old man who had only known the feel of his own hand on his cock, never even the lips of another man? Darren tried not to answer that one as he walked closer to the car, his face reflecting the uncertainty in his gut as Sam pushed himself out of the driver's side of the truck and reached out to give Darren a bone-crushing bear hug.

"Hey, boy, you're right on time. Fuck, I like punctuality in a pig. Makes me think maybe he's taking extra pains 'cause he's anxious to see just what I can do to him once I got him all to myself. Hey, let me get that suitcase for you. Fuck, boy, what you pack in there? Lead weights? You know, this is a clothing-optional campsite. Now, I know that all that weight can't just be boots and rubber butt plugs."

Darren had to laugh at the way Sam's words came out: as free-flowing and unfiltered as his back-and-forth on-line messages had been. It was as if Sam knew implicitly that Darren was as innately shy as he was awkward in the presence of most strangers. From the moment they had begun to talk on line, Sam had taken the lead in their conversations, revealing things about himself that most people never admitted to, let alone discussed with total strangers, even ones in a M4M Unusual Kinks chat room. It was that openness that had first attracted Darren to the man whose Instant Message he had answered reluctantly, and only after he had looked at his personal profile and attached photo that had impressed Darren so strongly on first sight. Darren understood what it was that Sam had seen in him during their first talks. Darren was an admitted submissive. He was a beginner and, therefore, open to being trained by a man whose own experience level exceeded anything Darren could have ever imagined. Later, when Darren had sent Sam the admittedly fuzzy and awkwardly-cropped photo his uncle had taken of him and his mother at the time of their last visit, Darren had almost panicked when Sam had not immediately responded to it. Two days later, Sam had finally sent him an Instant Message the moment Darren had signed on the computer. Sam had told him how his own computer had crashed and that he had to get a new hard drive in the end, delaying his response to the photo and e-mail. Sam had told him that he had liked what he had seen, but that he would like Darren's looks even better if he could let his hair grow a bit longer and fill out the angularity of his admittedly thin face with a moustache and beard. Darren had done as directed and now, in person and soon to be in the flesh, Darren had understood by the warmth of the greeting that what Sam saw was more than just acceptable to him.

"Damn, boy, it is so good to finally meet up with you. What's it been, boy? Two years?"

"Three, Sir," Darren responded, adding the word "Sir" out of respect and aware of the heat it generated in the mind of a man like Sam.

"Three? You sure about that, boy? Seems like a whole lot less than that. Anyway, that's more than enough time for any man to have to wait to get a piece of pig ass. So you're going to have to make it up to me for waiting all that time real long and hard, boy. And speaking of long and hard, I can see that you haven't been lying about what kind of meat you got there between your legs. I always did like a man whose dick walks three paces ahead of him. And while we're on the subject of big dicks and sex, let me ask you something....you packing from the other end like I told you?"

"Yes, Sir," Darren responded quickly, relieved that his dick had gotten hard enough for it to tent out the front of his pants and give Sam something to take the attention away from the rest of what was there to see. "I've got the plug in there as you instructed. I nearly climbed the wall that last mile heading here. Every pothole sent that plug almost up inside my brain."

"Yup, that's what it's supposed to do, boy. No use wearing it if you can't feel it in your mind as well as your body. And speaking of bodies....fuck, boy, why didn't you tell me that you got one that makes my tongue want to go head to toe and everywhere in between? You know what long and lean does to a man like me? Makes me want to shove you in the back of that pickup truck and pound your butt hole till it cries out to the moon for me to stop."

Darren wanted to tell him he had never said much about his body type because he had never thought that it was the kind that would set off any sparks that could be used to light fires in his hole. But instead of saying anything, Darren just smiled back at him, glad that he could see some telltale rising between the legs of a man who he knew had fewer inches to show off than he did, but a hell of a lot more that made up for whatever he didn't have there.

"Of course, you'll look a whole lot hotter once you get out of that geek clothing," Sam added as a postscript. "No offense, boy, but those chinos might show off all that dick meat I know you got packed there, but they don't exactly do anything to make a man want to plant his mouth on them, like leather pants or jeans, or absolutely nothing between you and the fresh county air would."

As usual, Darren was disarmed by the way Sam never held anything back. The man took plain speaking to whole new levels, especially during those incredible phone conversations where Darren had plugged his hole with a newly-purchased toy while Sam did the same, while both rotated on their chairs as they brought their dicks to the logical conclusion of all their verbal spewing.

"Anyway, you won't be the only one there looking as green as a jolly giant with a pine tree up his patootie. My buddy Jake's brought a boy he met in a chat room same as I did with you. Jake already had his new boy tied up to a St. Andrew's cross with his butt impaled on eight inches of hard rubber. You should have seen the look on the boy's face. Talk about your first-time angel staring up into his first look at Paradise. Almost got the boy singing the Hallelujah Chorus while his Master slammed his boot onto his butt plug. Anyway, you'll get to see that first hand soon enough, unless Jake's already got the boy doing something else equally twisted.

For Darren, just sitting next to Sam while he drove his truck down the narrow dirt road that led to the secluded campsite was akin to being willingly abducted and taken away to an alien planet. So far, all that he had by way of comparison to anything like the campsite was the replicated back rooms he saw on the fisting DVD's he had been purchasing for the past year. He wondered if the campsite would resemble the world of those DVD's, with hyper-muscled guys taking men's hands up their wide-open assholes, while others sat on dildos attached to chairs that they could be strapped into. So many of the men who had on-line profiles that proclaimed their love for fisting also listed hot looks and hours spent in a gym pumping their bodies into shape. Many had the photos to back up their claim, including claims for having dicks that would make their meat as sought after in the world of fisting as their hands. Sam had claimed to have a respectable six inches between his legs, more than enough dick for a man like Darren, who had never had the chance to find out how that compared to most of the available men out there. Sam also had a well-defined body that had entered its early forties with enough gray shading his hairy chest to make any man look at him and automatically whisper *Daddy* into his ear. And Sam also knew how to use everything he had to the best advantage. He wore a form-fitting tee shirt that showed off his well-sculpted pecs and nipples, made larger after years of hefty pulling and sucking. His legs were encased in well-worn jeans that gave Darren some idea of how beautiful the butt would be once it was exposed to him and available for licking and possibly even fisting. As he rode next to the man who had opened up so many possibilities for him, it was hard not to stare at the man driving or look down at the heavy duty boots pumping the brake, their surface glistening with traces of the last spit shine from a boot-hungry boy, who had licked it to an almost reflective polish.

"Go ahead, boy," Sam said as he watched Darren sneaking peeks at him. "Check it out all you want. You can even help yourself to a handful of this boner I've been popping for you. You'll be tasting it soon enough. Just like I'll be tasting that oversized pod of yours."

Darren blushed a deep red for having been discovered. But once they came to a stop sign outside the parking area to the campsite, Sam slowed the car down and reached his hand over towards Darren's head and tousled his dark blonde hair the way any Dad might do to his boy.

"You know, I like you boy. I especially like you all green and groin-hungry and waiting to be made into the kind of boy any man would be proud of to have walking three paces behind him. I always got a rise out of working with beginners, molding them into my kind of fuckers….men who can get as sick and twisted as I can get and not be ashamed to be there with their mouths and asses filled with whatever fits into them." Darren knew just how wide the parameters of Sam's sick and twisted mind could be. He had told things to Darren that he said he couldn't tell to a lot of other men: things that Darren had to admit were pretty far out even on the edges of kinky sex, but that he could understand, and with some help, learn to indulge in as much as Sam had hoped he could. And Darren had to admit, that with the truck now heading towards the sign announcing the campsite and his hand still cradling Sam's rock-solid cock, he did not feel as much trepidation as he thought he would once they were parked and it was time to begin the descent into that world of kink that awaited.

"Okay, boy, let's you and me get out. It's a bit of a hike to the cabin. I expect that Jake and his boy will be there playing as usual. You'll like Jake. He's almost as sick and twisted as I am. I told him that he might get a piece of your ass once I've laid claim to it for myself. Maybe swap boys with him if he's not so green-eyed greedy like most Masters with a new hole to play with. Like me."

As he spoke, Sam moved his hand on Darren's backside, his open fist forcing the imbedded butt plug deep inside his hole, just as planned. Even when they began to walk down the pathway towards the first row of tiny cabins, Sam kept his hand there, as if it was needed to keep the rubber plug well up inside Darren's still aching asshole. It made walking awkward, but it kept a smile on Darren's face, even when he stumbled on an exposed root and Sam had to quickly catch him before he fell face forward. It was a moment of awkward embarrassment. But the moment they came through the front door of the small cabin that they would be sharing with Sam's long-time fist buddy, Sam dropped Darren's bag onto the ground and pushed Darren's body into his while he leaned his head down towards Darren's face and forced his opened mouth to accept his twisting tongue. Once they had tongue-kissed for what seemed like a full fifteen minutes, Sam let go of Darren and opened up the door to the tiny cabin, revealing the almost stagy rustic ambience, complete with hand-made furniture and a deer's head hanging ominously on the wall between the large king-sized beds.

"I know I'm a handful for a first-timer like yourself, boy," Sam said as he laid Darren's suitcase down in front on the bed nearest the front door. "I never was one to pussy-foot about what I wanted. And right now, you are what I want, fucker. So don't expect me to woo you with flowers and candy-grams. I know what I need and I go after it, boy. And I know that's what you also need, boy, even if you don't fully know it yourself. Just remember, there's nothing you can't say to me, even if it's to back off. We're all about experimenting here, you and me. I don't own you. Not yet, anyway. So if it doesn't work out between you and me, you're free to look elsewhere. And if I need to do some exploring myself, I'll tell you in no uncertain terms. But even if I do go with others, I would still want to take you along so you can see what there is to see and do by way of kink. Now, about those clothes. I figured that I would wear just a jock and a harness and a couple of wristbands. I know you don't want to go bareassed, at least not just yet. But you've got to do something to show off that piece of meat you got waiting there for me and anyone else who needs it. So, if you got some shorts, that would be great. And if you feel comfortable enough to go bare-chested, that would be even better. But I understand if you aren't ready for that. So I got you a tee shirt by way of an introductory present from your Dad to you. I'd like you to wear it, but I know you might not be ready for it. Anyway, it's yours for the keeping."

Sam reached over to the distressed-wood nightstand and took out the shirt he had gotten for his on-line buddy once he knew that Darren would be joining him at the fisting weekend. He held it open; its sleeveless openings intended to show off well-muscled arms, which Darren knew he could never display for Sam or anyone else for that matter. Emblazoned across the front of the shirt in bold white letters was the message "Sam's boy." Darren smiled at Sam, aware that there was more than just the intended purpose of advertising his ownership of his boy that had caused him to select just that particular model tee. It was something they had talked about extensively on-line, something that Darren had rarely mentioned to others, few of whom had ever been as open to broaching the subject as Sam had seemed to be. Seemingly aware of what was going on in Darren's mind at that moment, Sam moved closer to Darren, his outstretched arms slowly reaching towards Darren's shirt as he began to undo the row of buttons at its front. He continued to stare into Darren's starkly blue eyes, Sam's bearded face reflected in those eyes almost too painfully handsome for Darren to contemplate as one that had just kissed him moments ago. Then, with one quick movement, Sam removed Darren's shirt and revealed the naked torso while Darren closed his eyes, as if afraid to see it reflected in those of the man who stood so close to him.

"Fuck, boy. It's as beautiful as I imagined. You, boy, are what I have been looking for, for a real long time. Wear the tee-shirt or not, just looking at you now, I got what I hoped for with you and then some."

Darren looked down at his bare chest, the mounds of nipples that Sam had encouraged him to develop almost as large as he himself had hoped they would someday be. His chest was as smooth as he had known Sam's to be hairy. It was lean and with a flattened stomach that gave way to a patch of pale blonde hairs that topped a dick now fully erect to its maximum hugeness. But it was not the dick that Sam stood and stared at. Nor was it the left arm that seemed as likely target for some future tattoos as they had talked about. It was the right arm that held Sam's fascination, or what there was of it. Unlike his own, it stopped at the elbow line, with a knob of rounded bone at the base that Sam had known would appear almost like a cock head....as if Darren needed anything more by way of obvious dick meat.

"I'll wear the tee shirt for you, Sir," Darren said. "And thank you for buying it for me," he added, even though the knot in his stomach told him that his words did not fully match up with the feelings that inevitably came with having to reveal the one part of his body he had never wanted to expose to anyone. But he knew that exposing it was not something he might have any choice in doing, since it was the one part that could excite Sam in ways Darren could never fully understand. And that, and not his own shame at having been born with nothing below the elbow of his right arm, was what mattered the most if Darren was to give himself over to Sam as he hoped he would. Even when

Sam touched the stump of his arm and raised it and his left arm above his head, he had to close his eyes for fear of not seeing in his friend's eyes acceptance of how mismatched both limbs were. When he did open them up, after Sam had slowly pulled the sleeveless tee shirt over his head, he still was not fully convinced that Sam was not repulsed by what he saw. Sam seemed to understand what was going through Darren's mind at that moment. He ran his hand across the chest that now proclaimed the body as belonging to him. He traced his fingertips around the hardened mounds of tit meat that he knew he would have ringed for the boy if ever he did own him as much as he hoped to. Then, as he almost read Darren's thoughts while he pinched the nipples through the cotton fabric covering them, Sam spoke once again.

"Remember how I told you I didn't want there to be anything unsaid between us, boy? Well, I wasn't joking, boy. You know about as much about me as any man can know without the benefit of having been in bed with me. You know how much I love your being an amputee. You know I intend to prove that to you, whether here between just the two of us in the cabin or outside in the play area where everyone can see."

Darren could almost accept Sam's devotion to his being one-armed. He understood that he was not the only man out there with that particular kind of fetish. But the stares of so many people as he walked by them with the under part of his sleeve pinned at the elbow joint had made him want to keep what lay underneath covered as much as possible. Sam had understood that. But he had also understood how much that was also a part of why Darren still lived at home with his mother, why he had been so reluctant to give in to the opportunity to fully explore his sexuality with others as kinky as himself, and why, even now, he seemed frozen in one spot as he stripped out of his shapeless slacks and pulled on the shorts that at last exposed his surprisingly well-formed legs. At Sam's insistence, he also reached into his suitcase and pulled out the pair of logging boots, whose long series of laces would have been torture for any one-armed man to tie in place. Instead, he grinned up at Sam as he reached down and pulled up the zipper that had been inserted into the side of the boot. He stood up quickly, having to admit that he loved the way the boots hugged his legs and seemed to give power to his stride.

"Now you look like Sam's boy," the older bearded man said as he let his hand massage the lower back of the man who would be his for the long three-day weekend. "Wish I could make you see yourself like I see you right now, boy. With a little work, I could make you understand that a man doesn't have to have the face of a model or the body of a porn star to be firecracker hot. And yes, you are hot, boy, maybe not in the way the magazines say a man should be hot. But hot enough to make me want to brand my name on your butt right here and now. Anyway, there's plenty of time for that. Right now I think you need to take a deep breath and start getting those sexy legs of yours in motion.

'Cause I don't know about you, but I am hungry enough to eat a boy, and if there's one thing you don't need, it's to have another chunk taken out of you. And the only way I am going to get enough in my belly is to go to where the food is. Not that I don't consider you a worthy meal...."

Darren smiled back at the man whose ease at dealing with his insecurities and even his disabled state was something he had almost never encountered. And as Darren passed a full-length mirror strategically placed opposite one of the large beds in the room, he had to admit that he looked far better in shorts than in khakis and that even with his arm stump exposed, the black tee seemed to show off his taut leanness to its best advantage, almost making him pleased with what was reflected in the mirror.

"Yeah, take a good hard look boy. Start learning to see what I see there."

What exactly that was, was difficult for Darren to imagine. He knew that he was passably good looking, that the scraggly blonde moustache and beard he had managed to grow during the last couple of weeks at least gave him a sort of backwoods charm. But no matter how hard he tried, he could not quite seem to see his arm stump as anything other than something to stare at and even pity the man attached to it for having to go through life with.

"You know, we all have our cross to bear, Darren. Your being born like that is just yours. So you just have to get out there and make the best of it." His mother had said that to him every time he would begin to feel sorry for himself and wonder just why not all of him had been formed in the womb. What she often left unsaid, but what he often felt as he listened to her misguided encouragement, was that he, in turn, was her cross to bear. Perhaps that was why part of him still felt guilty for leaving her alone in the house over the Labor Day weekend, when others would be out in their backyards barbecueing. And it didn't help any that as he and Sam walked through the winding path that led to the main house and dining area, Darren could smell what most likely was ribs and chicken slow cooking on an open grill, all of which he knew his mother loved almost as much as he did.

"Well, this is it boy," Sam said. "Home for the next three days. The kitchen is to the left, the dining hall is just past the main door. The bathroom's just on the far end of the dining room. No need to worry if there is enough for everyone to go around. Nobody's going to scream and haul up any skirts if you head to the Ladies' room. Of course, there are some around here given to wearing kilts. But that's a whole different kink. Anyway, there are picnic benches out back, which is where I was hoping we could head to eat. That's where they keep the barbecue pit. We're still a bit early, but I imagine that if we want to get us some good seats, we better start parking our asses in them. I also have a feeling that Jake and his boy will be back there somewhere. I thought they'd be fucking in the cabin, but I guess not. You'll like Jake. He's a real little pisser. And I mean that literally. If you ever want to see the meaning of 'raunchy' in the dictionary, it'll probably be under 'J' for Jake."

Darren knew that Sam was doing his best to make him feel as comfortable as possible. His talk had a nervous edge to it, as if silence would create a sort of mental distance between them that Sam might not be able to span once the distance between words became too wide to walk. Darren had to admit that he was relieved by it, that for a change someone wasn't just talking at him, like his mother seemed to do endlessly, but was talking to him, even trying to make him at ease as the words piled up.

"And by the way, boy," Sam said as he placed his hand on the small of Darren's back, "feel free to tell me to shut up if your ears start to turn numb from listening to me. You wouldn't be the first to tell me you like me better sucking on dick 'cause at least I can't talk with my mouth full of man meat."

Darren had to laugh. "I don't mind your talk. And Sir, thank you. Not just for bringing me here. "

"No need to thank me yet, boy. I haven't done a thing to you or for you so far, at least not what I hope to do to you and for you."

Darren knew that they both knew better. But Sam wasn't about to let the conversation get serious by mentioning that just his being there alongside Darren was easing the pain of walking by rows of seated strangers who might be judging him for no other reason than for what he had not been born with.

"Well, I don't see Jake here either," Sam said as he stopped just where the picnic tables began. "Maybe he's in the pool or already sampling the play room. Anyway, how about those seats over there? That ought to get us first in line for the eating frenzy. And speaking of eating….I recognized a couple of buddies of mine I usually get into some group play with before the weekend's over. I'll let you meet them later. You can decide for yourself if you want to join me in feasting on them or not."

Darren watched as a couple of hands popped up in greeting while Sam returned the gesture. Like Sam, most of the men already at the tables were taking full advantage of the clothing-optional policy. Some wore expensive leather cod pieces studded with nail heads that made Darren wonder what would happen to any mouth that tried to go down on them. Others, like Sam, wore well-used jock straps, revealing what seemed to be the complete range of dick sizes from barely average to almost as massive as his own. Still others wore regular underwear, some of which were strategically torn in the rear, revealing butts that Darren understood were as well-filled with plugs as his own was that very minute. Most men seemed to be there in groups of at least four or five, with only one or two couples by themselves. But more important, and far more interesting to a newcomer to the weekend fisting scene, the men who were there seemed to cover about as wide a range of physical types as cock sizes. Most were in their mid-thirties to late forties. Only a handful seemed to be much younger, with at least two who looked to be barely eighteen. Their bodies ranged from big bear-sized to obvious gym bunnies, which was more the kind that Darren had expected to find, instead of the variety he actually was seeing. Darren was also surprised to see that some of the oldest men, including one who had to be well into his sixties, had some of the best bodies. One in particular had the obvious look of a man who had been honing his physique for more years than some of the people there had actually been alive. But it wasn't just his body that caught Darren's attention. The man also looked like he would actually be the kinkiest one there, with a series of weights pulling down on his incredibly huge dick and balls that made Darren almost wince as the man stood up and it was revealed.

"That's Kirk," Sam said to him as the man with the weighed-down crotch smiled back at him. "Kinkiest fucker you ever want to encounter. See that muscle-stud over there near the kitchen entrance? That's his lover, Tanner. Boy turns twenty-one this weekend. Kirk's got a special party planned for him. Kirk's a professional piercer, and by the time Tanner leaves, there'll be more rings attached to his body than there are trees in the forest."

Darren stared at the future pincushion. Immediately, he recognized the same kind of perfect face and body that he had seen in dozens of professional studs who posed for the magazines that Darren liked to drop his load for. He also saw the way Tanner moved over towards the considerably older man whose body already looked like it reflected every fetish he had been able to conjure up in all the years he had lived on the earth. Immediately, the muscle boy reached down for one of the massive rings that were stuck through his partner's chest. He held it in his hand, and then slowly tugged on it as the older man reached out to the boy's pouch-covered crotch and provided enough of a vise grip on the boy's balls to make his face twist as he worked his partner's tit.

"They love to show off. Hell, if I had a body like Kirk's and a stud puppy like Tanner, I would be showing off every chance I got. Not that I don't have my very own stud puppy in you, boy. Anyway, that's just a sample. I expect that Kirk will be spending a couple of hours making sure his boy is in a sling. Kirk's a real pig when it comes to showing off. Those weights he's wearing….that's just a sample. And that boy of his, well, Kirk's got a contract that says that the boy's body is his to use and modify as he sees fit. I guess we should take one last look because if I know Kirk, he'll be turning that boy into the Illustrated Man before the boy hits twenty-two."

It was not hard to see why someone so incredibly perfect as the young muscle stud might want to place his soon-to-be-inked and pierced body in the hands of a man like Kirk. Even at a distance, the aura of power that surrounded the older man was hard to miss. The group of men who sat on either side of him seemed little more than window dressing as the boy called Tanner was forced to move under the table, where he would remain at the feet of his Master until that Master was ready to feed him scraps from the table. Darren was about to comment on the scene of submission and domination unfolding two picnic tables away from them. But as he opened up his mouth to talk, another man caught his attention: one very different physically, but with the same aura of absolute power about him. Darren stared at the barely five-foot-two frame approaching, with its huge barrel chest that sprouted a maze of hairs like Sam's, slowly and sexily turning grey. He looked across at the man, moving towards their direction the legs that were as powerful as any he had ever seen, exposed in all their hairy massiveness as an overstuffed jock pouch kept the cock well hidden inside.

"Hey, there's Jake. Fuck if he doesn't look like that dick of his just got sucked off."

The thick fireplug of a man smiled back as Sam stood up and grabbed his own jock-covered crotch and screamed at him, "Hey, asshole, the pork's been here waiting for you to chow down on. Where the fuck have you been?" Jake returned the greeting by flipping his still hard dick out of the jock strap, revealing an overhang of foreskin that was as red as the patch of crotch hairs that stood out at the base.

"Where the fuck does it look like I've been? I've been getting my foreskin chewed on and not by you, asshole. And if you're going to offer me any part of a pig for eating, you better make it pork butt, fucker. I just had all the chops I can stand for one night." As he spoke, another man moved beside him, a much leaner and taller man whose looks vaguely resembled Darren's, and who walked as if apologizing for every step he took. Darren recognized the regulation dog collar around his neck and the pricey leather shorts that contained enough D-rings for the armbands he wore at his wrist to be attached to for restraining purposes. Darren also noticed that the boy did not respond to what was being said around him, taking cues only from the man who grabbed at the leash attached to the studded collar and pulled him behind himself as he walked over to where they sat.

"I'm Jake," the red-headed fireplug said as he reached his leather banded hand out to Darren. Darren took the hand in his own, aware that Jake had probably been told that Darren was one-armed, which would explain the lack of surprise registering in his face. "Darren, this piece of trash is boy. Boy, say hello to Darren."

Immediately, the boy got down on all fours and moved his face into Darren's brand new boots. He held his face close to the shiny leather surface, and then began to lick it off as Jake pushed his own boot into the boy's plugged butt and ordered him to suck. Immediately, Darren recognized a well-trained tongue, one that did what it was told and that took no notice of where it was heading, whether on a grungy boot or into a ripe asshole.

"Good to meet you, Darren. Sam told me you were a piece of ass. Fucker never lies. Okay, boy, get your ass up here like a good dog. I was showing the boy his kennel at the playroom. Told him I expect to keep him there while I pass my hand around to any pig who needs it up inside him. Also told him that when I get good and ready to let him out of his cage, I want to see his ass parked on the other side of the glory hole wall, sucking up anything shoved into his face."

Darren didn't know which to react to more, being told by Jake that he was a piece of ass, or the image of the boy working a glory hole where any cock would be fair game for his mouth to service. Instead, he just smiled back at Jake as the man planted his well-rounded ass down at the picnic table, with Sam on the other side and the boy waiting for the okay to take his place next to his Master, Jake, as Darren slid next to his Master, Sam.

"So what do you think of Camp Fist Fuck?" Jake asked Darren. "Must seem like a whole other planet to someone just getting into the scene. But I got to tell you, if you're going to explore the world of wide-open asses, you couldn't have a better guide than Sam here. Fucker taught me everything I know, which is a hell of a lot. Got me when I was strictly bottom. He knew that I really wanted to be a Top but well, I figured that with a small dick and small hand, I'd have to be the one opening up my ass to anyone a lot bigger on most counts....which is just about every man here. But he taught me that I can still open up my fuck hole to a fist and be in charge, so before you could say 'anal douche' I was running in both directions. Took a while, but once I learned how good it was to have a man's butt hole hugging your hand, I started only topping guys out. Found out that a lot of them can only take a hand my size. Anyway, I got to give the devil his due. Sam sure made good Daddy material out of me for guys like the boy here. Haven't needed to give up my butt hole to get a good cocksucker down on my meat in years. Told the boy that if he's real good, maybe Sam'll give him permission to take on that big dick of yours he's been bragging to us about for the last three years. Hey, boy, you gonna work Darren's meat like I showed you? Damn, you should have seen the boy when I first met him. Fucker had the worst gag reflex I ever saw. Had to suck on ten-inch dicks myself to show him how to control his mouth muscles. Now that pig's able to take more in his mouth what he's been taking up his wide-open ass."

Darren realized that most of Jake's conversations were rhetorical, that he could outtalk Sam any day, which was probably why they had never become partners - only friends and fuck buddies. But as he talked, Darren realized that there was more to Sam than just the expected layers of control and kink. Sam always seemed to be teaching something to a man as he worked their bodies while he gave their minds some unexpected twinges as well. He could tell by the way Jake praised his ability to control and give over to his own piggishness in equal doses that Sam was not just the sex machine most men had hoped he would be. Even as Jake talked a blue streak, his conversation punctuated with equally blue rhetoric, Sam never lost sight of the fact that Darren had come to the camp at his urging, to see if he could ever become part of a world that he had remained for way too long just on the edge of. As Jake and Sam exchanged banter, Sam slowly let his hand slip down into the front of Darren's shorts, his fist grabbing hold of what Darren had always assumed to be his only asset that he could offer up to men who could and would do far better by way of sex partners. He already knew that Sam had claimed bragging rights to that dick by allowing for the possibility of Jake's boy to claim it for his newly stretched out throat. Darren could tell from the look on Sam's face as he talked that his hand was duly impressed by the fact that his hand could barely hold Darren's meat now that it had swollen to its full thickness. But as the hand slowly came out from inside the shorts and moved across Darren's shoulder, Darren was equally pleased by the way the same hand gripped the spot on his shoulder blade where Darren hoped to one day etch the name of the man he called his partner in permanent ink.

"I'm glad to see that some of the old crowd has come back," Jake continued. "We had some pretty bad weather last year and guys left moaning and groaning, and not just from having their buttholes filled. It's also good to see a couple of new faces. That piece of stud meat Kirk brought is someone I would like to get in the sling for a couple of hours. But I did promise to give all of my attention to the boy, at least until he's had enough and needs to soak his hole in a bucket of ice. And speaking of hole, I think that his is just about as well done as some of that meat they better start serving soon. Why don't you pull that plug out boy, so I can see just how it's coming along?"

With not the least twinge of shame or self-consciousness, the boy stood up and pushed his upper body over the picnic table. More than one man stopped midway in his conversation as the boy spread his asscheeks while Jake moved his hand to the spot where the plug rested, then slid it out by the knob of rubber that prevented it from going dangerously far inside the opening. Darren looked into the boy's face as it was removed, the combination of pain at its removal mixing with the relief of the pressure its constant presence had sown. Some men from across the room began to applaud, still others held their ovation, as the boy was ordered to sit back down and did so with his asscheeks half on and half off the hard wooden seat. All around them, men were beginning to move towards the line that had formed in front of the barbeque as it was announced that the food was ready. Sam asked Jake if he wanted him to bring him back some food, and once he said that he did, both Sam and Darren joined the slow-moving line. With a crush of bodies on either side of him, Darren once again felt the familiar pangs of self-doubt as men talked to each other, groped between legs for what they would later claim as their second meal for the evening, and introduced their latest partners to their playmates from past years.

For Darren, there was the usual awkward moment as some men moved their hands out to him automatically to be shaken. Some accepted his left-hand shake easily and with little awkwardness. Others stared at the arm stump while trying to decide if it was okay to reach for it or just do the more easily achieved bear hug that seemed to break a lot of ice down to a slow melt. By the time they neared the source of the amazing smells assaulting their nostrils, Darren's head swam with names he would never remember as he was handed a tray and a paper plate and napkin filled with plastic cutlery. He held the tray tightly, aware that for him, balancing it was a must, and that anything he could not manage to hold on to with one hand would have to be gotten later once the line thinned. Sam seemed to understand his dilemma. He grabbed an extra plate and filled it with mounds of food that he would give to Jake, with some scraps saved for the boy. He reached in for a couple of cans of beer and added them to the tray, its weight already wresting more than one joking comment about his true piggishness from some of his buddies. By the time they walked back to their own table, Sam was tired of saying, "It's for Jake. Fucker's too busy to grab his own eats." But when they finally got to where they had been sitting earlier, Darren understood why Sam had been so wiling to serve as waiter.

As they pushed the trays of food onto the painted top of the table, Darren reclaimed his place next to Sam on the bench. Jake and his boy seemed to be sitting there awkwardly, which prompted Darren to look behind them. It was then that Darren noticed that Jake had his left hand pushed up inside the part of the boy's butt that hung over the seat. Just the top of the hand was visible as the boy's face wore a look of contorted pain and pleasure, each one coming in equal doses. Without missing a beat, Jake moved his free hand outward and grabbed at a can of beer, whose pop-top Sam had pried open. He took a swig and held it in his mouth, then, pushed the boy's face into his own as he spewed the contents onto the boy, who accepted it as if it was the most natural thing in the world to have beer spit onto him from his Master's lips.

"I told you Jake was a sick fuck," Sam said as Darren stared at the man and his boy open-mouthed. "Wait till you see him in action later. Man can rim your intestines out of your asshole with that pig mouth of his. Says it's just to get his boy's ass relaxed enough to take his hand, but we both know better. The man loves ripe hole any way he can get it."

"Yeah, and guess who taught it to me to take it like that? All I can say is, Darren, I hope that Sam gets to work on your dick and ass as good as you're expected to do him. Then you will truly be able to say that you've been cock sucked and ass eaten by a Master, and not just a fist fucking Master. Now, how about passing me a rib? My stomach's growling. And you don't want to be around me when I can't get to the food in front of my face. And don't worry about the pig next to me. Boy doesn't get to eat until I get to eat."

Sam handed him the plate he had gotten for him. They all ate in silence, with Jake swigging on more beer and spitting it out into the boy's open mouth after he had chomped on a rib or a sauce-covered chicken leg. Once he was sated, Jake began to hand-feed the boy, who sucked spilled sauce off his Master's hairy chest while his hole continued to be filled by the man's small, but decidedly powerful, fist. When the round of eating had stopped and everyone who seemed to want seconds and thirds had gotten their due, one man walked up to the front of the dining hall and planted his boot-clad feet onto the platform where a microphone was waiting. He was a big man, almost as tall as he was wide, with his leather vest covered with souvenir pins from past biker runs and tree-like legs shoved into leather chaps that cinched at the waist and forced his sizable belly to protrude. He looked down at it and his leather jock covered crotch barely visible to him below. "Okay," he said. "Any of you pigs ready for dessert?" The crowd roared back at him, his leather gloved hands now massaging his leather pouch. "Well, tough shit. None of you get this unless my Master gives you permission first. Instead, this is what all you ass stuffers deserve." With that, a huge food cart was rolled out with an equally sizable cake sitting on top. Jake could barely make out the design etched in icing, but once it was tipped about one inch forward, he could see the traditional black and blue and boxed heart of the official leather flag, with a clenched fist coming upward form the lower right hand corner in flesh-colored icing. The crowd went wild as the man displaying the cake reached for a knife on the table, dipped it into a glass of hot water, and began cutting neat squares as he made certain that at least one square of cake was rubbed into his belly so that it could be licked off later, with the permission of his Master, of course.

"Now, for all of you out there who have never been to one of these shindigs, let me remind you of the rules. First off, nobody leaves unsatisfied. Second, park your attitudes outside your cabin door or tent flap. If someone doesn't interest you, have the courtesy to be polite about it. Third, we don't own this place. Piss in the urinals or in your partner's mouth, not on the fucking floor. Clean up after yourself. That means no guest towels covered in Crisco. We got rolls of paper toweling for cleanup. No loads shot on the walls and although some of us might look like bears, that doesn't mean we use the woods for crapping in. Fourth, the playroom will be open 24/7. I expect it filled. Fifth, I'll be in the first cabin to the left of the main house. If any of you pigs need to fill something up, my hole is ready, willing, and able. And yes, for that you don't need my Master's permission. Just leave tips in the empty Crisco can on your way out. Now, all you go out there and have the best fucking time you have ever had in your life. And remember, we got beer and snacks round the clock. You get hungry for ass, you come to me. You get hungry for bologna and beer, you come to the dining room. For those of you who might be up in time for breakfast.....what the fuck is wrong with you? I want you pigging out until the sun rises like a cock inside a slippery butt hole. Now, go take a fucking douche and get ready to fist your way into the Guinness Book of Records."

Darren knew just how extensive the preparations for heavy ass action could be. He had taken with him the metal snake that he could attach to the bathtub faucet and clean himself out well enough to have even his biggest dildos come away clean from an all-night session. He understood that some of those preparations might be performed for him by Sam, who was the one who had told him all about them in the first place. As he watched Jake stand up, his hand finally out of the asshole of the boy whose first spoken word all night long was a sincere "Thank you" to his hairy little Master, Darren heard Sam and Jake deciding who would get to use the bathroom first. In order to get it done quickly, Jake and the boy would pair up and make use of the facilities, while Sam and Darren waited in the bedroom for them to finish. As they walked back to their cabin, the man who had made the "announcements" only minutes earlier passed them by. He called out to Sam, his belly still wearing the cake he had smeared there. "Hope you can come by later," he said. "And hey, bring your pal." Darren stared at him as he moved up to another man standing nearby and let the man drop to his knees and begin to lick his belly, cake and all.

"That's Ed," Sam said to Darren. "He's been running the event for the past eight years. You ever want to see just how far a man-hole can be stretched, you go spend an hour or two with Ed. Jake and I double-fisted him last year. I've gotten well past the elbow a couple of times. I heard that he's taken a foot too, but I've never seen that so I can't vouch for its truth. If you want to know what you have to aspire too, just watch Ed in action."

Darren was familiar with all of the fisting jargon, the rituals like the inspecting of a man's fingernails for any evidence of anything that could cause damage to a man's insides, and designating key words that meant *stop*. He knew that rubber gloves were required and that boxes of them would be provided. He also knew that not all fisters used the old tried and true Crisco lube. As he walked with Sam into the cabin, he reached for his suitcase and began taking out the "kit" he had put together that contained some of the essentials for the scenes that he hoped would soon unfold. He would carry it with him to the playroom, just as most other men would do. As Jake and his boy moved into the bathroom and began their extensive preparations, Darren watched Sam as he, too, set aside the kit he would also be carrying. Then, as the bathroom door was locked and the water began to run in the tub, Sam moved closer to the man he hoped he could initiate fully into all of the rites of what some viewed as almost ritualistic sex.

"They won't be too long. I expect that the boy has already cleaned out, or Jake wouldn't have claimed his ass like he did. And Jake doesn't get fisted, not since that biker he met in Dallas sent him to the emergency room. So we have a couple of minutes to get better acquainted."

With that, Sam moved Darren towards the bed they would be sharing and claimed one side, while he watched Darren join him from the other side. Sam was once again fully erect, his cock head making a wet spot on his jock that Darren knew he would be sucking up soon enough. Darren's own dick revealed its full length through his shorts, urging Sam to grab at those shorts and pull them down so that Darren was naked from the waist down except for his boots. Sam stared at the hugeness of the dick that seemed to almost be compensation for the lack of a full arm. He wanted to suck it down to the crotch hairs, but instead slid alongside the boy and let his right hand reach out towards the stump of Darren's right arm. He moved his hand across its length, his eyes locked onto Darren's own eyes as he searched the boy's face for any traces of uneasiness that his caresses might be causing. He saw none. Instead, the boy closed his eyes as his face took on an almost beatific expression as Darren was touched for the first time in a spot he had never expected any man to willingly venture.

"Let me enjoy your body like I want to," he heard Sam whisper into his ear as the same mouth was slowly moved to where his hand had been seconds ago. Darren could feel his breath stop as Sam's lips moved across the shortened limb, the lips finally resting on the nub of rounded flesh that had always made Darren want to keep it covered. As he gave in to Sam's need to savor his disability, Darren reached out to Sam and let his fingers come upon the hardened mounds of tit meat he knew that Sam wanted him to work hard and soft in alternating doses. He could hear Sam's own breathing, deep and with as much passion as if his mouth had been on Darren's huge cock instead of his cock-shaped arm stump. Then, as he gave in to the kind of pleasure that he would never have imagined just the touch of a mouth to his arm stump could cause, he felt Sam's hands moving onto his ass as he pried the well-rounded cheeks apart and gripped the end of the plug that rested deep inside between the two melon-like halves. He felt those same hands slowly pulling the plug out, the pain of sudden exit always far more intense than the pain of entry. And once it was out, Sam began working first one finger, then another, and still another, until all three were deep inside him. He knew that it was just a prelude, that he would be expected to at least attempt to let an entire hand work its way up inside him. He wanted it. He wanted it just like he wanted Sam to continue to mouth his stump, like he wanted everything else other men had gotten so easily, but that he had rarely even attempted to go after. And as Sam worked his hole, his fourth finger sending a sudden rush of pain up through Darren's body, he coaxed him with his voice, as seductive as any he had ever heard.

"Look around you tonight, Darren. Take in what you see and learn from it. Think about Jake, little Jake who has a boy as hot as you as his slave any time he wants it. Think about Ed, who gets a man to suck food off of his big belly and has a Master who once won a leather contest. Think abut Kirk getting ready to have his stud boy tattooed and pierced. And think about all the other guys, a lot of whom will want your asshole riding their hands. Think about who and what they are and how what they have to offer by way of pleasure counts for more than how pretty they are or how many times a week they go to the gym. And there'll be more guys heading out here tomorrow, all kinds of guys who want nothing more than to open their asses or pry open ones willing to take what they can give. You can be one of them Darren. I want you to be one of them."

Darren let the words wash over him. He had no illusions about his looks, which he could make hotter with leather and rubber, but which would never be anything like the man who Kirk wanted to cover in ink. He could tell in a glance if a man was ready to accept him for being disabled, and he could go outside himself if the look in the other man's eyes was one of disgust, not resigned acceptance. He could take the kind of rejection he had been getting all of his life, sprinkled with a healthy dose of condescension and lame jokes about one-armed bandits or questions about how he had lost it, which was not what had happened. It had just never been there. He could understand how a man like himself would look to another area, like his asshole, by way of compensation and draw the attention there, like men with tiny dicks often did. But what he had seen so far was nothing that resembled a camp full of men compensating or intentionally drawing attention away from physical liabilities. What he saw with his own two eyes was a little man like Jake, claiming what was due him, which was a willing slave boy, even though the boy was ten inches taller than he was. Or Kirk with a lover almost fifty years his junior. He understood what Sam was saying, what Sam was doing; how he was leading his mind away from what he didn't have or what he could give. And as they remained in bed, Sam's hand partially up Darren's ass, Darren decided that he had only his inhibitions to lose, nothing more. And when the bathroom door opened and Jake and his boy came out naked into the bedroom, neither one seemed surprised to see Sam's lips attached to Darren's arm stump, just as no one seemed surprised that Jake's cock was as stubby as his body, and that the boy went down to suck on it the second that Jake sat on the edge of the bed.

"You two better get busy in the bathroom," Jake said as he leaned back on the bed and let the boy do his job. "I promised the boy a load before I plant his ass in front of the glory holes for a couple of hours. I also promised Ed some action."

Darren heard the words, all said as if getting his admittedly small tool sucked on by a boy whose own dick was more than just a sufficient suck. "And if either one of you need to drop a load, the boy's as good a receptacle as any. Aren't you, fucker?" The boy barked out the required, "Yes, Sir," then Jake barked out another command for him to get his mouth back down between his legs. By the time Darren and Sam were finished in the bathroom, the boy had worked down to Jake's boots, his face beaming broadly when Jake then pushed him off of the spit-shined leather, pushed him down on the bed and began to suck out the boy's open asshole with his outstretched tongue.

"And so it begins," Sam said as he retrieved Darren's shorts from the bed. "Well, I guess we better leave the two of them to it. Guess Jake'll be wanting us to leave the door open, just in case anyone wanders by and decides that they need some of the good stuff. Better get dressed, Darren."

Darren looked across at the men on the other bed. Jake ate out his boy's butthole with no thought about what role anyone seeing him suck on that wide-open cavern might assume that put Jake into. He knew that Jake was a Master, even with his mouth filled with boy hole. Just like Sam was a Master, even if he did want to sample every place on a man where a tongue could logically and even illogically go. "If it pleases you, Sir, I would rather go to the play area naked."

Sam looked down at Darren, his face beaming as he watched the huge-dicked man thrust his legs back into his side-zippered boots over the thick sweat socks he had gotten on one-armed.

"Fuck, boy, nothing could please me more. Well, I can maybe think of one or two things. But parading you around bare-assed....now that's a real chart topper."

Darren watched as Sam also got into his own boots, each one with enough laces to make him cringe at the thought of ever having to get into a similar pair. He held his breath as the man pulled his cum-stained jock strap back over his cock, the same cock Darren had become well-acquainted with after Sam held a nozzle to his butt hole so it could be cleaned out.

"We'll be right behind you," Jake called out to them as they left the cabin, the familiar sound of one man's tongue on another man's body resounding through the warm night air. That air felt incredible against Darren's bare skin as his cock moved from side to side as he walked, prompting more than one man to turn around and stare at it as it swung. "Fucking exhibitionistic pig," Sam joking called out to Darren as more and more admiring glances helped his dick to slowly rise.

"Thank you, Sir," Darren responded, his body entering the play area with his dick fully erect and ready for whatever action it might get. Sam grabbed hold of that stiff dick, his hand holding it tightly as he walked with Darren into the room where dozens of men were already beginning their night's activity.

"Welcome to the real world, fucker," Sam intoned, his hand still holding onto Darren's risen meat. "Now, let's show them what a one-armed boy from Plattsburgh can do."

The "playroom" was a freestanding structure that had been built to serve a myriad of purposes the groups renting the campsite might have needed it for. No doubt its original designers had not intended it to hold portable slings or allow for guests to set up a stage-like area that could be covered with rubber sheeting so that large groups of men could writhe naked, ass attached to arms, on its slick surface. Darren was amazed at how many men had brought their heavy-duty equipment, which might account for why so many of the vehicles in the parking lot were pickup trucks.

"Jake said we can go ahead and use his sling for a while. He'll probably be spending some more time in the cabin with the boy. Probably asked a couple of guys to join him there. Anyway, it's ours for the taking. Now, you want to toss a coin for who gets in it first or do you want to get your first taste of what it means to have a man's hand inside you?

Darren was well aware that Sam liked to get as well as he gave. But while Darren had lots of experience working his own hole with whatever was available to him, he had never even thought about working his one good arm into another man's stretched-out butt.

"I think I might claim first dibs on it," Darren said. "But that's your decision, Sir."

Sam liked the way Darren deferred to him. He understood that, as the older, more experienced of the two, it was only natural. But he also understood that Darren's need to submit was greater than his own could ever be. For Sam, doing things others considered bottom and, therefore, submissive, was an act of piggishness, not deference to the man getting the attention from his mouth or ass. He could never take orders like so many he played with seemed to do as naturally as eating and crapping. When Sam did choose to enjoy another man's body, it was his own decision and often made so that the recipient of all that attention in his own body could be rewarded for work that was well done. It was those traits that had attracted Jake to him. He had met Sam at a time when his own longings to be in charge of men's bodies had begun to take shape in his admittedly twisted mind. With Sam's help, Jake was now more of a one-way Top, much to the satisfaction of the many one-way bottoms like his newfound boy. Darren knew that most likely he too was destined to be a one-way bottom. But he also knew that Sam would help him explore both halves of the very kinky coin and decide for himself which position he preferred.

As Darren let Sam hoist him up into the leather seat of the sling and hook his booted legs into the straps that would hold him tightly in the contraption, he watched as, one by one, men of every shape and size also made their way into leather-covered slings. Darren watched from side to side as asses were displayed to the men who stood in front of the slings, rubber gloves on their hands, as they greased those hands and slowly eased them into the waiting holes of their captives. Darren knew that some of them used drugs such as muscle relaxers to get their holes to open wide without the accompanying pain of entry into an area not intended to take more than toilet paper. Some covered red handkerchiefs with poppers and held them to their noses while their asses were slowly but decidedly opened up to their full potential. Others, like Darren, chose to experience the unfolding scene with clear minds and bodies that would react strongly to any potential problems caused by taking on too much too soon. It was a tradeoff in pain that Darren was willing to accept. But Sam had not been so sure and had urged him to at least take a muscle relaxer. Darren had responded that he would never let anyone do anything to his body that he could not endure and even come to enjoy. Sam had admired him for that. But he also knew that it would make introducing Sam to the world of fisting a lot more difficult.

"I'll start with just fingers, boy. You tell me if it's too much and I'll stop. Tell me when you're ready for more, too. And remember, boy, this is supposed to be pleasure for you as well as me."

Darren stared up at the ceiling, its exposed beams criss-crossed with spider webs. Then he looked into Sam's face and smiled as he saw the look of concern on his handsome features. It was a good sign. He watched as the man across from him took a hit of poppers, then let the man in front of him shove his fist into his open rectum as his mouth formed a scream that was more theatrical than it was released out of pain. The man with his fist buried up inside his hole wore a look of triumph on his face. Darren understood that his having taken so much of the man's hand in one steady motion was a mark of a well-experienced and well-sought-out fistee. Darren knew that he would not be putting on such a carefully rehearsed show. As first one finger, then another made its way up into his open fuck hole, Darren could sense that taking flesh and bone was a lot more painful than taking a rubber dildo. His mouth formed a silent "O" as the configuration of the long fingers and jutting knuckles presented a new kind of sensation for his previously unused ass. But as he moved his face to his other side and watched as one small-built man began to open his butt to a man almost twice his size, Darren smiled as he realized that the smaller man, too, was a beginner. As their eyes met, the look in those eyes said that they both understood that their first fisting would always be the one best remembered, and that being able to watch another begin his career would only add to the pleasure at finally having what they both desperately needed.

Sam had known the man whose ass was also being opened up for the first time. He had spoken to him on-line and had passed his name on to the man who was now claiming his butt cheeks. He had told the man that he had already committed to bringing Darren to the campsite as his personal boy for the weekend. He also knew that his buddy, who stood almost six-feet six-inches, loved working on guys whose bodies he could tower over. Both knew that their mismatched bodies presented the kind of kinky contrast that some men there would find amusing; others would think it was yet one more layer of added steam to what was admittedly a kink that was incredibly physical, but with unlimited potential for a hot mind-fuck.

It was the mind-fuck of having a one-armed boy that gave Sam the kind of mental stimulation he knew that he would one day let Darren in on and help him explore and accept as part of his physical presence. Sam knew that some might question the attraction that Darren had for him, others might write it off as something akin to having a portable sideshow in your sling. A few men, like Jake and the man next to him working his own odd-looking private pig, understood that it was the difference, coupled with the act of fisting, that so many saw as being way too over the edge. That made being with Darren so much more compelling to a man like Sam than having a perfectly proportioned muscle stud. And then there was Darren's dick. It stood at its full height across Darren's flattened stomach, the equally impressive nut-sac almost blocking the way to his rosebud ass opening. Sam moved in closer towards that anal canal, his face locked onto Darren's as the boy stared back, then turned towards his left to watch another beginner cope with the sudden cramming of a hand into his manhole. Sam had hoped that both boys could watch each other, understand that they were both giving their Top men pleasure in ways that few other submissives ever could. But Sam had more to show and teach to that other couple and others in the room. As he slipped a third finger into Darren, he lowered his face onto the dangling nuts and popped both balls into his waiting mouth. He watched as Darren snapped back to attention the moment his nuts were encased in Sam's throat. He stared up at the ceiling as the man working his ass began to let his tongue roam over the smooth surface of the dangling balls. Then, as Sam slowly began to pull back with those balls locked in his jaw, both Darren and the man lying in the sling next to him understood that the lanky body in the sling was meant to experience not just pain in the ass, but throughout every part of it that held the key to its sexuality.

"I won't do anything to you that you don't want done, and the minute it gets to be too much, you signal me to stop."

Darren remembered those words as the ache in his balls began to match the ache in his ass. He knew that he was nowhere near his threshold. But he also knew that what Sam was doing was not just something he needed to do, it was also a test of Darren's ability to take what was given to him and in his own mind turn whatever pain came with it into pleasure. He knew that soon Sam would release his nuts and move his mouth onto his dick and begin to slowly suck on every inch of its admittedly impressive length. He stared over at the man in the sling next to him, the cock between the legs of the man lying there belying the myths about all short guys being hung like beasts. Even with his ass now beginning to open up to the admittedly huge fist of the man controlling it, the cock remained soft in its small state, making Darren almost embarrassed to be staring at it. But the man in the sling knew that it was natural, especially for a man so impressively well-hung himself, to look between his legs, to want to wonder what it was like to live with and be gay with something so small, just as the tiny-tooled man had to wonder what it was like to live with one arm that stopped just above the elbow joint.

"You see that little dick on that little fucker," Darren heard Sam say as his nuts were released from his mouth, "I told that boy that I was going to suck that baby dick for him just like I was going to suck on that slab of donkey dick you got between your legs. And I told him that I would be enjoying that tiny prick just like I was enjoying yours, 'cause that's the kind of twisted sick fucker I am."

Darren understood that *sick* and *twisted* were two euphemisms in Sam's vocabulary that equated with *hot* and *as good for the brain as a whole head of broccoli*. He also understood that if Sam called him a "crip" it was not a pejorative because "crips" were what he liked best and the kind of men he sought out on the Internet, just like Darren sought out older, more experienced, men like Sam.

"Nothing about Sam's what most men are about," Jake had said to Darren when Sam had gone to get some more beers and Darren was left alone with him and his boy. "Fucker's taught me more about myself than any shrink could do in ten years of me lying on a fucking couch. Later, when Sam was in the bathroom, Jake had turned to him and said exactly what Sam was now showing him was a fact. "You know what they used to call 'sexual healing' in the 1960's? Well, Sam's a one man EMS team. Fucker called me his 'runt' the first time we met. Said it was the nicest thing he could say about a man, then turned his ass around and proved it. Told me I was no more a fucking bottom than he was, and that if I wanted to prove it to myself, I should use his ass to experiment on. Fuck, it was like giving a ten-year-old the keys to the candy factory. Fucked that pig hole for more than twenty-four hours straight. And when I finally got my pants back on, I knew that the man I fucked was no more a bottom than I had thought I had to be. Man gave me his ass to prove a point: to prove that just because I was a fucking runt I didn't have to act like I was one. So that's the kind of man you got there, Darren. You be the fucking pig whore you need to be. But you remember that everything he does to you he can take and then some. You're gonna come away from this shindig more trained than you ever hoped you would be and in ways you never expected you would be either."

Darren had to admit that Jake had not been lying. With Sam's mouth now on his massive stiffer, the pain and pleasure that surged through his body was like nothing he could have ever imagined he would know. Sam had managed to get most of his fingers into the steadily stretched opening that Darren had already trained to accommodate beyond anything he had ever dreamed of. He knew that others were watching Sam work his magic meat at the same time, impressed that the boy had as much dick meat as he did open asshole. But when Sam let go of his cock and slowly moved his mouth onto Darren's leg, Darren understood that there was more to learn that just the pleasure of being fisted and cocksucked. Sam had stopped his lips just at the top of Darren's boots. He had held his hand straight out in anticipation of the final thrust into the butthole that cradled his fingers. And as Sam moved his lips onto the surface of Darren's spanking new boots, Darren felt that hand sliding into his gut, taking with it any remaining doubt about his future as a man in a sling.

It was not so much the searing pain that seemed to block out any conscious thought in Darren's mind. It was the sight of his Master licking the surface of his boots that seemed to make that first entry ever into the depths of his bowels far less painful than he could ever have imagined. "Ain't no sense wasting good dick meat or a hot fucking pair of boots or even the feet inside them once you got a boy's legs that far up in the air," he had said to his buddies as they had sat around planning the events that would unfold over the three-day weekend. "So you can call me a fucking bottom if you want. I know what I am and I'm really happy with that. For me, it's called adding layers to a mind-fuck. And the sooner you start loosening up and fucking with your brains and not just your dicks, the sooner your boys are gonna start realizing that their asses didn't come with a manual telling them what a fist-fucking pig bottom should be acting like."

He had said it to incite the men in the room who still adhered to the rigid notion of who's on Top and who's on bottom. He knew that he could go on to add something about sucking on a midget or licking a pair of ears that jutted

Dumbo-like from the face of a man nobody would ever call handsome because of those projections. But he knew that except for a few, like Ed or the man who was now standing next to him fisting his small-built novice, his words would have little effect. "Why is it that with something like kink….that most everybody out there thinks is sick and fucking perverted…guys still want to write rules about it and judge others for doing things their own way?" It was as rhetorical a question as any, and eventually Sam just let the conversation die down to an uncomfortable lull as they moved on to deciding the designated breakfast, lunch, and dinner times. Later, Ed would move up to him, place his hand on Sam's backside, and tell him that all that frustration wasn't worth it, that some men in the room still wanted to give out stickers that would say who was Top and who was bottom with color-coded stick-on dots deciding their fate. "Might as well ask me to wear a sticker that says *Hello, my name is Sam. I am a Top fister*…. only I also like to have my ass plowed too, as long as you don't think I'm your fucking slave boy because you got your hand up inside me….and by the way, I also get off on guys missing arms or legs and if you've got a hot pair of fucking boots you can expect that I also want to lick them off, which, by the way, only makes me boot hungry, not somebody's boot boy." He was preaching to the choir with Ed, who gave every inch of his big bulk over to his Master, had to ask his Master permission to be used by any other man, but who fed his piss to his Master when the man said that was what he needed, and never thought of the well-built stud as anything other than his Master, even when the fucker was drinking his piss from a beer bottle Ed had filled with it.

Darren knew that it could be years before he could ever sort out the entanglement of political and sexual motives behind the men who were at the weekend campsite. Some had come only for the fisting. Some, like Sam and Jake, saw fisting as part of their overall cache of kink, albeit a pretty important part. Darren could look around the room from his position in the sling and see that there were some men being tied to tables containing rows of hooks around their padded leather surfaces. One was screaming out with the pain as a hot wax candle slowly dripped onto his exposed genitals. Another man was being lead into the room by a chain attached to his leather dog collar that rested beneath a full leather mask that kept his identity a secret. Darren knew that most likely, in an adjoining area, Jake's boy was sitting on a wooden bench, sucking off cocks that were pushed through a strategically placed hole that allowed men to pass their meat on to the willing cocksucker on the other side of the hole. Darren lay back on the sling, his ass almost ready to take the final plunge of Sam's fist into its insides. He slowed his breathing as he had been told to do. He let his mind wander to a place where he knew that he could almost abstract his mind from what his body would soon be feeling. He looked first over to the man in the sling next to him, his tiny dick still soft as his partner punch-fucked his hole and made him scream out to the point where he needed to be gagged. Then Darren moved his gaze back towards Sam, his mind now poised to give him what he had come there to take and receive in equal doses. He moved his head back, so that the ceiling once again filled his line of vision. Then he nodded his head, the signal that he was ready to be brought into his next phase of learning.

He tried to be the kind of boy Sam would want him to be. He tried not to scream out like the man to his left had done. He tried to take the almost unbearable pain of entry into his rectum in stride. But as the knuckles on Sam's tightly held hand slipped past an opening intended for expelling, not receiving, he could hear his own voice roaring out above the din of the room as that hand slid down so that the wrist was buried deep inside his bowel. Not even the stopping of any movement inside his ass could ease the pain. He tried to remember the agreed upon word that would make the pain stop, but it was lost to him as his mind seemed to move to a spot above his body, where it had to ask what the fuck he was doing in a room where men were inflicting pain on each other and justifying it with a statement that it was what the bottom wanted. Darren did not want the ache. He did not want the disassociative feeling that he had felt for so long in a body that he had never really wanted as his own. All he wanted was to be a part of something. And now, with his body once again failing him, he wanted this latest venture towards that goal to end.

"Let your mind go, boy. I know it hurts. Remember, it's your first time. But if you make me take it out now, you might never again want it back in you." Darren heard the words, as if through a fog. But they did little to comfort or change the fact that his asshole was on fire. "Stop being such a fucking martyr, boy. Take a hit of poppers." Darren felt the glass vial against his nose, his stomach churning as the unfamiliar smell assaulted his nose. But he breathed in deeply as Sam told him to, first with one nostril closed, and then the other, so that the fumes soon crept up into his nose towards his sinuses. He felt the faint throbbing at his temples that slowly grew as the amyl nitrate did what it was intended to do, not for kinky-minded men, but hospital patients. And once its full effect was known, Darren could feel that what had seemed like unbearable pain seconds before was now a still healthy dose of ache, but somehow was more bearable. Sam smiled back at him, aware of what was happening inside his body. "Let me take you all the way home, boy," he whispered as he handed the capped bottle to Darren and told him to take more when he needed it. Then, as Sam gauged just how relaxed Darren now was, he moved his fist a fraction of an inch inside Darren's wrap-around fuckhole, gauging by the look on the man's face just how much more he was ready to endure.

Darren felt the movement inside his asshole. But it now seemed as if it belonged to someone else's butt, someone who was still somehow attached to him, but who could take the brunt of the pain for him and only allow Darren to feel what was necessary to let him know that the hand was still there. And as Sam stared into his face and watched his mouth slowly relax until it formed the kind of smile he had seen on his own face so many times, he began to slowly move his hand in and out of Darren's ass as he slathered more lube onto the exposed wrist. Sam looked at the man who he now could claim he had fisted. It was not the most beautiful face he had ever stared into. It could appear gaunt if the man attached to it ever dropped more than ten pounds of weight. But the nose was strong, as Sam liked men's noses to be. And the eyes were as blue and expressive as any he had ever seen, only closed shut right now as they would have been expected to be at that moment. He liked the way the blonde beard and moustache seemed to grow out of the skin as if it were patches of crabgrass instead of a well-manicured lawn. And he liked the hair on the head, a bit longer than was currently in fashion, but which added to the almost redneck charm of the man whose ass his hand was filling. And there was that dick, as huge as any he had ever tasted, with balls to match. But it wasn't the cock meat that held his attention as he began to move his hand gently in and out of Darren's now accepting fuckhole. Sam held his hand secure inside the boy's butt, then moved his other hand towards the one spot that caught his attention more than any other. He reached for the arm stump that the boy in the sling seemed so ashamed and embarrassed by and caressed it as Darren's eyes quickly opened. He understood the look in those eyes and moved that hand so that he could help the boy push his upper body upward on the sling while his ass still held Sam's fist tightly in place. It was a movement that sent new pain through Darren's body, but it was pain that he didn't need any chemicals to ease. And as Sam continued to fist him and as the pain eased once he held his repositioned body rigid, he let his eyes remain open as Sam leaned his head in towards him and let his mouth rest on the end of his arm stump.

Suddenly, there was no question in anyone's eyes why the man lying in the sling was the one that the hot older man had chosen as his fist toy. It was understood why the small-built man lying so close to him would later get his tiny cock and balls buried in the same mouth, so that nothing would be visible except a freshly-shaven crotch. It was even understood why the same man's size seven feet would also be licked, when all the other foot fetishists in the room seemed to be begging for size twelve and over. And as Darren lay there, his open hole now understanding why men would train theirs for years to take what he was finally experiencing first hand, he knew that nobody watching Sam suck on his arm stump could ever forget that he was an amputee from birth, but that at least one man thought that lacking something that others had was an asset, was something that could be turned into just another fetish for a man who already had more than most men's share of kinks and yes, twists and sicknesses. And some, like Jake, who had now entered the room with his boy in tow, understood just how happy a man Sam was at that very moment. But others thought that stump sucking was a bit too weird even for them. Still, others would make a connection from their crotches to their brain and realize that Sam was onto something more than just a missing part of a man's body. But it would be hours before they would fully understand and see just what that connection had wrought.

****

"Having fun, boy?" It was as rhetorical a question as any he had ever been asked. Once out of the sling, Darren had thanked his Master profusely for doing to his ass what he had been hoping for a long time someone would do to it. As the spit on the end of his arm stump had begun to dry, Sam was still inside Darren's hole, removing his hand when the pain became too intense, then pushing it back in as Darren rested and recovered. The man in the sling next to him had also been pumped for almost an hour, his ass then given over to Ed's Master as the bulked-up man walked into the room and told his slave to go over to the glory hole room and get himself some dick to eat. Darren had watched the muscle stud fist the man, who he had never expected to see a tattooed and muscled forearm attached to. Then, before Sam could claim it for his own, the man had clamped his lips down on the soft dick between the boy's leg and continued to pump his hole while he finally got the cock erect enough to shoot a load of cock cream down his waiting throat. Darren's own dick was at that very same point of ejaculation as Sam watched his friend fist and suck at the same time as if it was stud meat down his throat and not something an inch or two less than the five inches his own partner could supply him with. Sam saw the look on Darren's face and had begun to take hold of the pole between the man's legs and started jerking on it while he held his lips poised at the humongous mushroom head. He knew that once spent, the pressure in his ass would become unbearable, and Sam would have to submit the boy to the considerable pain of removal of his hand from his hole. But Sam needed the boy's load. And the boy needed to shoot it. So as he began to punch-fuck the ass he was still letting his hand ride, Sam told Darren to let his load out so he could wear it on his face and then plant the streams of drying spunk onto Darren's countenance as well.

It was not just the words about his being made to wear his own load that forced the juices up and out of Darren's widened piss-hole. He, too, understood how painful the exit from his ass would be. He knew that once out, he would need to let his hole recover before he could even contemplate one more fist, either Sam's or someone else's, to get back inside him. But it was the thought of the sight of Sam, the handsome Sam with his slowly graying hair, covered with his own cum, that finally let that load fly out of his cock as he screamed out with release. Even after the face that stared back to him was completely engulfed in the white sticky mess his pent-up excitement had generated, Darren could still feel his cock throbbing as still more juices leaked out, and Sam grabbed at them with his hand and smeared them first across his beard, then across Darren's face.

And Darren had to admit that the feeling of a man's fist leaving his now aching butthole was almost as unbearable as the feel of it going inside him past the knuckles for the first time. And so Sam had held him gently as he withdrew his hand from his asshole, the loud final pop of its slide back into the air sending a stream of trapped lubricant with it. Sam rushed for paper toweling and wiped up the mess from Darren's ass and the leather seat beneath it. He grabbed more towels and cleaned his own face off, then Darren's, once he had helped him out of the sling. Darren wobbled back onto the floor, as if the simple act of fisting had aged his body thirty years. He felt his sea legs slowly gain back their footing, while the ache up inside his butt continued to remind him just what level of piggishness he had achieved in the past hour and one half. He held on to Sam, in part to steady his body, in part because he knew just what a gift he had been given by the man. Sam seemed to lap up the attention, his face almost beaming as Darren's nakedness gave him a prize big-dicked boy to show off. But it was another simple gesture that almost made him want to cry out as he realized just how far he had helped the boy come. As they walked to the far end of the room where others as temporarily spent as they were congregated and exchanged lists of their kinks and fetishes, Darren moved closer towards Sam after receiving some encouraging words about the quality of their performance. Then, for the first time in his life, Darren moved his right arm towards the face of another human being and moved it across the chin and cheeks as others might do with a hand, not the stump of an arm. Sam moved both his own hands upward and held the stump, kissing it gently as any lover might kiss the hand of a partner. Then he smiled back at Darren, a smile that was as sly as any other Darren had ever seen.

"We'll rest for a while, boy. That load you shot on me was a good two cumming's worth. Then I want you to get your ass back over to that sling. Only this time you're gonna do to me what I just did to you and then some. You ready for that, boy? You ready to give your Daddy's hole what yours took from him?"

"Ready…willing….able," was what Darren thought. But with his mind in a sexual cloud of a reverie, all he could do was nod his head and follow Sam back toward the dining room where they would get some more beer and chips and wait for their energy to return, which was soon enough.

"Hey, everybody's talking about your performance," he heard Jake say as he dragged the dog-collared boy over to where they stood eating. "Boy here did real good, too. Got every size and shape dick in that pig hole of a mouth of his that a man could possibly swallow. Even got a ripe ass or two shoved through the hole that he could eat out. I told him that if he was real good he'd get to eat both of your asses after you got 'em fisted good and hard. Boy likes sloppy seconds. Fuck, boy likes anything I tell him to like. You should have seen his face when he saw you sucking on your own boy's boots. Told him he'd have to do a hell of a lot of pig-outs before he ever got me to do the same to him. But it's not impossible, not by a long shot."

Sam understood that Jake could never be as public a pig as he could be. But he also understood that in private, like in a cabin with his best buddy who he could never put on airs with, Jake could let loose and do to his boy what Sam might do to Darren. The boy would have to accept that and not wonder if that meant that there was any shifting in their role-play. There wasn't. Jake would always be Jake; a little Top man who once thought he had to be a bottom. And that suited Sam just fine. Jake looked damn fine covered head to toe in Sam's spit as his former mentor licked his hairy little body head to toe. Those little feet, held for hours in calf-hugging boots, would retain just enough funk to remind Sam that Jake was a hot, sweating sex machine who would always give up every inch of his body for licking, cementing their friendship in ways that most bonding never could encompass.

"Anyway," Jake began, "Like the man says…the show's not over, not by a long shot. And in case I have to remind you what depths of trough wallowing I am capable of….let me say right now that you ain't seen nothing yet."

Darren liked the way Sam bragged about his abilities and exploits, aware that someday he would be telling others about the fisting virgin whose arm stump he had sucked off while a room full of fist freaks had to realize that there were layers of kinks even they could never have imagined. "I don't know about you, boy, but I think I am rested enough to make a return to the play room." Jake muttered something about playing the Triumphal March from the opera *Aida* and having his boy spread rose petals in their path, but Sam said that all that was needed was him heading in first, with the boy on his leash following from behind so he could get a good look at both their asses. And that was exactly how they made their way back into the play room, Sam once again moving towards the sling he had set up there hours earlier, which was next to the one he had borrowed from Jake to break Darren in while his own was also handed over so that a beginner could be tested out in it. But Darren paused as he headed towards it and wondered if it was his body that Sam wanted in it or if Sam would claim it for his own. "So, now that you've seen and felt how it's done," Sam said, as if reading his mind, "it's time for you to see how good a fist fucker you can be. Call it second stage training or fair switching. It's now time for my hole to get some good hard use, boy. So, why don't you get your stuff ready, and I'll get my ass in the sling, which is where it belongs."

Darren reached down for the leather bag that contained grease and his own sizable collection of ass toys. He walked to where the rubber gloves were kept and took out a single glove. He knew that Sam would forego the toys he had brought and take, instead, his left hand that had fingers long enough to let anyone looking at them know that the dick might match inch for inch, which, of course, it did. Darren knew that Sam's ass was already well lubed, but that he would expect Darren to add more grease to it so that it could accept what was about to be thrust inside it. He watched as Sam positioned himself into the sling, a lot more than he had done with only one hand working to give him leverage. He stood there as Sam looped his booted legs into the strapping that would hold them him place. He had never licked boots before, but understood that Sam might want him to do it as he pushed his hand into the admittedly more practiced and stretched-out ass hole. When the man whose hand he could still feel affecting the state of his own butthole was in place, Darren pushed the can of grease under his arm stump and held it tightly in place as he moved to place his glove hand into the sticky white lube juice. Sam smiled back at him, then reached for the grease, most likely to make it easier for Sam to dip his own hand into. But instead, Sam reached over and removed the rubber glove from Sam's hand. Then he reached down into his own bag and pulled out a packet of condoms, condoms about twice as big as any he had ever seen. It was then that Darren realized that Sam wanted him to fuck him; something his stiff cock seemed to say it was more than willing to do.

But it wasn't his cock that was the intended target for the rubber. As Sam ripped open the packet with his teeth and pulled out the almost laughably big folded ring of latex, Sam reached for Darren's arm stump and began to roll the rubber down onto it. Men around them paused in their sex acts to watch as the cock shaped stump was sheathed and there was no doubt in anyone's mind what was going to happen next.

"You comfortable with this, boy? Cause if you're not, we can stop right now."

Darren looked around at the faces, some mesmerized, others not sure if their stomachs were ready to see the variety of fist fucking that was about to unfold in front of them. Then Darren saw Jake and his boy move closer to them, the boy as wide-eyed as if he had been asked to walk into a room with a wall full of cocks dangling out of glory holes. The boy watched as Jake moved his hand onto Darren's back and began to stroke it gently, his gesture saying far more than just words could. Darren looked to his side and saw the man who had been in the sling next to him also move forward, his small, spare frame contrasting wildly with the well-muscled stud who held onto his shoulders. Darren watched as the man who had as much a virgin fist hole as his own minutes ago reached down for his tiny dick and began to stroke it into what was as much of an erection as he would ever achieve. And he watched Sam as he drank it all in, knowing that some brains were in gross-out mode at the thought of seeing a stump fucking about to take place. Others were about as pig happy as their porcine namesakes as they realized that they were about see a mind-fuck even their sick brains could never have conjured up. Still others would be trying to place what they were about to see in some sort of perspective or trying to figure how they could get the one-armed man to do them like he was about to do to his partner for the weekend. And a couple, like the small-dicked novice whose stud protector seemed to enjoy pushing his stiff prick up against his freshly-opened butt hole, fully understood that there was magic in the mating of the mismatched that few others could ever fully understand.

But it was none of that which mattered to Darren. It was the sound of his mother's voice in his head saying "Now, Darren, you have to realize that a boy like you has limits, and that if you try to go beyond those limits you are bound to come away sorely disappointed. I can send you to the same school as all those other boys and girls in town who will probably just make fun of you and call you names....or I can send you to the special school where all the other little boys and girls will be just like you." But they had not been just like him. And they had no problem making fun of him and calling him names, as if they didn't share something that would forever label them, too, as cripples. But that was not something he could ever tell his mother. And when the boys on his block asked him how he was doing in Basket Weaving 101 all he could do was respond, "Just fine, thank you," and walk away to the sound of their laughter.

"Sir," Darren said to Sam, his voice cracking as he spoke, "you don't have to do this to prove anything to me. I think I already understand that I can be as much a part of what goes on here as any man."

Sam stared back at him, aware that their conversation could be overheard by others. "Fuck, boy. You think I'm doing this for you? You have no fucking idea how many years I've thought about meeting a guy like you. Any of these assholes here can give me a fucking fist. You, boy, can give me something to fuck my ass and my brain at the same time. But if you're not ready to do it, I'll understand."

As Sam stared into the face of the man who had just swallowed his whole hand and thanked him for it afterwards, he watched as an ear-to-ear grin moved across the boy's face, as if a light had just been turned on from within. "You think I'm some kind of idiot? Me, miss an opportunity to work your hole like you worked mine? Damn, I might look like a backwoods boy, but I know an opportunity when I see one. You, Sir, are going to get your insides tickled like you never had them tickled before."

For the first time, Sam realized that he could not just look at Darren as some sort of novice who was soaking up every new twist of mind and body like he was Billy Sponge-Pants Bob with his body filled with Crisco instead of soap. For Sam, it was a relief. He loved the banter of domination and submission. But when the lights were back on and he and a boy were no longer playing out elaborate mind and body games, Sam wanted to relate to his boy as an equal: as a man.

"Fuck, boy. You punked your Daddy good and hard….acting like you didn't know what I had in mind for that hot stump of yours. Fuck, boy, now, fist me good and hard like you know you can do. And if I scream out for you to slow down, it means I want more. I like putting on a good show for my buddies. Let's see if you can match me act for act."

Darren had watched as more men gathered around them. Maybe it was because most had started playing at about the same time and most were ready for a break, which included watching others play their favorite game of stick it to the butthole. Or maybe it was because Darren offered up another twist on the old game of pin the fist on the fuckhole. Either way, Darren knew that part of him was enjoying the kind of attention the slow greasing of his arm stump was getting. As Jake moved in behind him, the hot fireplug of a man ordered his boy to go down on his knees and suck on Darren's dick while he stump-fucked Sam, Darren knew that he would never have to go back to jerking off to pictures of men in magazines. With his stump now completely greased up towards the sparsely-haired pit, Darren smiled back at Sam and aimed the knob end of it towards his open fuckhole. He felt the intense pleasure of having a well-taught mouth latched onto his dick as he leaned forward and stretched out Sam's gaping rosebud with his free hand. He started at the circle of pink flesh that he knew any seasoned fist taker could open and close like it was a fish mouth staring back at him. But he didn't need the gyrations of a butt pucker to get him going. His dick was being sucked, and as he brought the end of his arm towards Sam's hole, the look on the face of the man about to get his hole invaded was more than enough to allow him to begin the slow ascent into an asshole more willing than anyone could ever have imagined to take something it had never taken before.

"Better use those poppers like you told me to do," Darren said as his stump began to slide into the kind of open anus that had taken more than one fist at a time while its owner's mouth had been filled with ripe cock meat. He knew that he might never get another man to open up to him in quite the same way. But as Sam let his nostrils fill with the musky-smelling vapors, he knew that he would take full advantage of the situation and put on the kind of show he had only thought that pumped-up porn stars could ever give. He heard more than one man around him saying how he wished he was Sam at that very moment, the gaping hole that was his ass widened by the inch as it resembled a tunnel being bored out from solid granite. But it was not rock that Darren's sensitive arm stump was feeling. It was the insides of a man who had used his own tunnel digging techniques to open up his mind. And once the knobby end of his stump had disappeared into Sam's butt and he could see the almost beatific smile on the face of the man taking it, he stopped pushing, so that the anal opening could get used to accommodating his forearm. Then he resumed claiming more space inside the bowel.

Darren scanned Sam's features for any sign of intense pain or resistance and found none. All he saw was unbridled ecstasy, coupled with the realization that his feat was being watched by some of the men he had been the most intimate with. And as Darren pushed his stump to the point where anyone coming into the room for the first time would have thought that there was a full arm up inside the man's gut, Sam had him stop the steady probing into his butthole and asked Darren to just let his stump rest where it was. Darren gave in to the feeling of having his dick worshiped while his hand was holding on to the insides of a man who had also claimed his own butt. Darren could see that Sam had reached the limits of his endurance, that his breathing was shallow, and that no amount of poppers would alleviate the ache in his open asshole. Darren knew that he had to pull back just a little, that there was time enough to make him take the full upper arm again. But as his own dick came close to filling the mouth of a man who he knew only as 'boy,' Darren watched as Sam finally pulled his cock out from under the piss-stained jock strap that held it in place. Darren wanted that dick again. He leaned closer, his lips brushing the cock head that sent groans escaping through Sam's parted lips. He knew just how close the man was to shooting. Knowing that, and also knowing that Sam's tolerance level for his arm stump was beginning to wane, Darren pushed his mouth onto Sam's cock and let the full length of its six-inch shaft tickle his larynx while his own huge dick made the boy at his feet gag with pleasure.

"You want the boy to take your load?" he heard Jake ask as he held on to Darren's back and caressed the exposed butt crack. All that Darren could do by way of acknowledgment was nod his head, as he hoped that Sam would also release his load at the same time that he fed his spunk to the boy. But the boy was too talented a cocksucker to allow for any delay. Darren felt his entire body begin to shake as the force of his own load shooting out from his piss slit sent his arm stump up inside Sam's hole, so that all the man in the sling could do was scream out as his own spunk went flying into the mouth of the man who had impaled him.

"Get it out, boy! Get it out," Darren heard Sam scream. Darren understood the urgency and complied, although its swift exit from its surrounding anal wall would be more painful than he could ever imagine. Sam knew that and gripped the edge of the sling; his teeth tightly clenched as he felt what seemed like a battering ram move down his butt hole and exit with a stream of pinkish colored lube grease. For a second, Darren panicked as he realized that blood had been drawn. But Sam reassured him that it was just a capillary that had seeped its juices onto the gloved stump and that it would heal quickly, leaving no permanent damage except possibly for an ass now stretched to take more than any hole in the room could manage to take.

Neither the boy sucking Darren off nor anyone watching had been prepared for the intensity of a man being stump-fucked while the man with the stump creamed up enough cum to repopulate half the Eastern Seaboard. As Jake lifted his boy up from the floor, he could see just how thoroughly his face had been plastered with spunk and just how satisfied the boy had been at taking the kind of cock most pigs only dream about. And once a couple of other loads were added onto the already cum-slick floor, the men who had watched the event and would talk about it for one year when they hoped it would be repeated at the next fisting get-together, began to move away from the two men who had provided so much entertainment. Only Jake remained, with the boy by his side.

"Well, Sam's finally got what he's been talking about getting for the past twenty years. And the boy's finally gotten enough dick meat so he could go home with a smile on his face. And you, boy," he said to Darren, "have gotten the kind of reputation that will keep that arm of yours up to the elbow in asses for the next fifty years. Now all I have to do is let the boy drain my dick and we can all say that we are happy pigs...for now at least."

Sam knew just how temporary Jake's satisfaction would be. He also knew that his little stud buddy would get that dick drained by as many men who could eat between his well-muscled legs and not get out all there was inside him. But Sam also knew his own limits, and the boy called Darren had pushed him dangerously past them. Still, he knew that now that the boy had proven just what his body could offer up by way of kink to any man willing to explore it, Sam understood that, for Darren, the weekend could be an endless round of stump-fucking and getting his own butthole filled as many times as he needed it.

"Damn, you did me in, boy. Not sure I can do much more tonight. So, if you want to head off to try some other guys out for size, you're welcome to do it."

Darren watched as Sam pushed his body out of the sling, the ache in his ass obvious as he tried to take a couple of steps but had to stop before he could get his body limber enough to head towards the front door. He saw that others had been inspired, and that all of the slings were once again occupied, including Jake's, which now held a boy waiting for him to take advantage of his having been worked up so thoroughly but still not allowed to touch his cock.

"Guess you can rent out your sling for the rest of the night, Sir," Darren said as he moved alongside Sam. "Anyway, I think I ought to quit while I'm ahead as well. I was thinking that maybe we could take advantage of the cabin being all ours for a while. I'm not sure that I will be asking for my ass to get worked on again....or my dick for that matter. But Sir, this boy would be honored if he would be allowed to lick his Daddy head to toe and everywhere in between."

"On one condition, boy," Sam responded. "You get as good as you got just like you did all night long. No use quitting on a formula that seems to work so well."

It was what Darren had hoped to hear.

"So, you think maybe we should grab a couple of beer bottles? Because I might not be able to shoot another load like I just did. But fuck, I can always piss."

"On me or in me?" Darren responded, knowing that either one -- and especially both -- was just fine with him.

"Fuck, boy, you think I'm some kind of pervert? Pissing on a man? Making him drink my piss? Damn, boy. You better let me get us a fucking six-pack. Maybe two. On second thought, let's get three. Hell, you can carry a six-pack, you're not a fucking cripple. Three six-packs ought to do us for a while at least," Sam said jokingly.

Darren smiled at Sam, who always seemed to be one step ahead of him in the kink department. But it wasn't the words about getting into some hot piss play that caught Darren's attention. He had plainly heard Sam tell him that he was not a cripple, even if only in jest. But now that the word was out between them, it seemed to take on a far different tone than when people at work had used it to describe him, albeit behind his back. He knew that to some people out there, his being one-armed would always define who and what he was. But at least he also knew that for Sam, being that 'cripple' most men saw him as, was not the barrier to hot kinky sex he once thought it would be. He had to smile at that thought, aware that this was one that few men outside of the ones who engaged in kinky sex might ever understand. But for Darren, that was enough. Somehow, he also understood that he had now become a part of that world, where kink compensated for a whole lot of liabilities and perhaps even made those liabilities seem even more alluring, because they were what most men avoided. Somehow, to Sam, and to some extent to Darren himself, kink and crippled seemed to fit, well, like a rubber glove on a fist about to open up a man's greased-up fuck-hole.

"And maybe when we're finished, we can open up the front door to the cabin," Sam added as they headed back to the dining hall. He was ever willing to test the limits of someone freshly exposed to the kind of heat he was capable of generating, hoping that it would be understood, appreciated, and made part of any future scenes together. "It lets the fucking bugs in. But it also lets the pervs and pigs in as well, so the trade-off is well worth it. That is, if you think you can get into a having a revolving door policy. I should have warned you that not many of us get a whole lot of sleep when we're here. That's why some of us stay a day later, after the partying ends, to catch up on some Z's before we have to head out. Anyway, it's your choice, boy."

Darren grabbed for a six-pack of beer and held it in one hand, then reached for another and tucked it under his arm stump. It was cold as all hell up against his skin, but at least he could say that he was carrying his own load. Sam smiled back at him as they walked to their cabin, aware that he would have to refocus some of his thinking about Darren. "You know, Sir," Darren said, almost hesitantly at first. "It's occurred to me that I've been sleeping for over thirty years. So, if you think it's in my best interest to service anyone who comes through the front door, well, I'll trust your judgment. And I was hoping to thank Jake for letting his boy suck my dick by doing whatever he wanted me do to him by way of appreciation."

"That's your decision to make, boy," Sam answered. "I know Jake'll be real pleased to have a crack at your crack. I might need to tongue out his fuckhole while he rams your butt, though. Man's got the sweetest ass….well, the second sweetest. Damn, just listen to us. We sound like a fucking married couple who spend their nights watching nothing but porn and thinking up new ways to spice up fifty years of non-stop fucking."

"Fifty years of non-stop fucking sounds real nice," Darren said as Sam opened up the door to the cabin, and he quickly dropped the pack of beer under his arm onto the edge of the bed he would share with Sam. "Anyway, at least a long weekend's worth. That is, if you want it."

Sam dropped the six-pack he had been carrying onto the bed and pulled out a bottle that he held dangerously close to Darren's waiting butt hole. He rubbed it against the ripened rosebud, forcing Darren to jump as the cold up against his hot ass made his body instinctually react. "Hey, I thought I was going to get that second-hand," Darren added as Sam popped open one beer and began to swig.

"You will, boy, mouth and ass," Sam responded. "Mouth and ass."

****

"So, you guys have a good time?"

Ed was once again at the platform facing the rows of tables that filled the dining hall. It was far more crowded than when Darren had first arrived, and he had watched Jake push his hand up his boy's hole while he ate. As hoped, Darren had thanked both Jake and the boy for the expert cocksucking Jake had made the ever-submissive slave boy give him.

"What's that? Doesn't sound like much of an enthusiastic response. Not by a long shot. Now, I know that some of you have had more than your fill of fun this weekend. And to be honest with you, I have to admit that for me, this year's haul was a record breaker. I bent over this morning and found four watches, three rings, and, yes, one rhinestone bracelet stuck up my butthole. Well, I never said that I was picky about what kind of gloves the person fisting me was using. Rubber, embroidered kid leather....it's all the same. And in case any of you still want to leave some trinkets with me, the play space will remain open until 3PM. I know that some of you will be staying on until tomorrow morning. For those hardy souls, breakfast will be at 9 AM and checkout time by twelve noon. We'll be working the clean up crew once breakfast is over. So, anybody who wants to wipe away some of their DNA, that would be a good time to volunteer. Otherwise, I'm bringing in the CSI squad and every one of you fuckers who didn't get to use my hole is going to be arrested for negligent homo-cide."

The crowd groaned. Ed knew that he was slowly running out of material. "Now, on a more serious note....I want to say that this year's attendance was at an all-time high and that we collected over $3,000 in charitable contributions. So I want to thank all of you in advance for contributing to my rectal reconstruction fund." More groans filled the air. Darren knew that the money would be used towards causes that the group routinely backed. He also knew that Ed could have no complaints about the personal use of his asshole. It had been on display in the playroom the night before, with its admittedly cavernous interior filled to the hilt with the muscled arm of his partner. And that was only for starters.

"Well, as much as I want to stay and chat, I have work to do. But before I go, I want to seriously say that it has been great hosting for all of you guys. You are an amazing bunch of men. And in times like these, being able to be with others who think that sexuality is something that everyone should be entitled to enjoy to the fullest has only made the group's leaders even more committed to expanding the event like, well, like you know what. And now, before I get my ass out of all of your faces, I want to ask once again -- did all of you guys have a good time?

This time the response was a unanimous roar. It was easy to see that not just Ed was warmed by what he was hearing. All around the room, Sam could see that there had been some new pairings, while other more established couples like Kirk and his muscle stud had managed to engender new friendships and play partners. His own relationship with Jake had somehow deepened as Jake used the techniques that Sam had taught him to spin a mental web around the boy he had brought with him who, hopefully, would be returning with him in the following year. Sam had the same hope for Darren, but knew that he would have to work with him slowly and consistently to bring him even further out of his shell. He knew that they would be meeting up again, perhaps at Sam's apartment, where they could explore the intensity that seemed to be growing between the two of them, even while they extended their sexuality to others who could appreciate their dynamic.

"You know," Ed said once the room quieted down. "I'm still not fully convinced that you mean it. So, this time I don't want you to just answer me when I ask you if you had fun. This time I want anyone who says 'yes' to raise his hand if he's sure. Okay? Now, I'll ask you one last time....did you guys have a good time?"

This time, the response was deafening. But along with the roar that was one of genuine appreciation for all the work that had gone into making the event the most successful so far, hands began to reach up into the air as well, more than one rotating to the left and right, not as some royal wave, but with the same motion used to push those same hands up into men's greased-up asses. Sam's was one of the first to raise his arm up, followed by Jake's as he, in turn, told his boy to give the fisting sign even though he had only been a taker and not a giver. And as Sam watched the sea of upraised hands showing their approval for the gathering of like-minded men, he moved his eyes onto one man who sat next to him and who had shouted perhaps louder than anyone else in the room. And he saw that it was not a hand that the man whose face was clearly etched with emotion had raised, but the stump of an arm that he now seemed to have no shame in displaying in its shortened state. And Sam knew that Darren, like any man in that room, had an absolute right to display his "hand" and move it in a corkscrew motion. But Sam also hoped that Darren would not just continue to use it on his own ass and the many other willing asses that seemed to be ready to accept it. Sam hoped that Darren would also use it on the rest of the world, telling it what it would get if it didn't include him in its share of what was due him. And even if Darren could not yet make the connection between claming an ass and claiming his birthright, which was his full sexual potential, Sam knew that every opening, anal and mental alike, took patience. He was prepared to be a very patient man. He knew that his patience would be rewarded. And with that thought in mind, he grabbed at the shortened arm of the man who had held it inside his butthole as they both let everyone in the room know just what an incredible time they had together, with the hope of more such times etched clearly on their grinning faces.

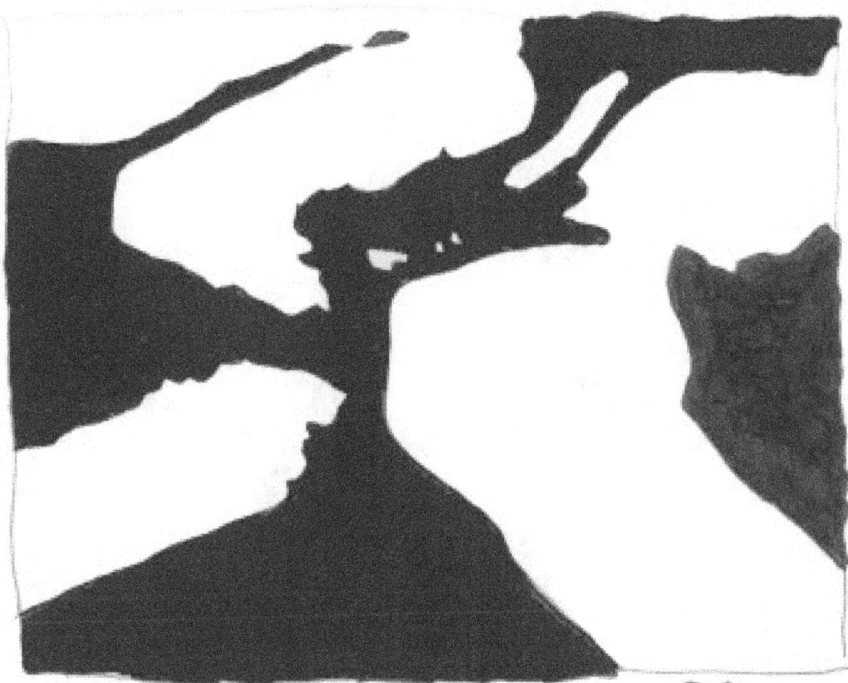

Ed Moore
2005

A Boner Book

INDEX

A

Acidophilus 13
AIDS/ HIV iii, xvi, xix xv, 9, 10, 11, 21, 31, 36
Arnett, Chuck vii, xi, xv

B

Baldwin, Guy xv, xxiii
Bales, Michael xiv
Bareback Buddies 40, 42
Bareback Raunch 40
Barracks, The (San Francisco) xviii, xix
Barracks, The (Toronto) 71
Bean, Joseph W. xv
Bifidopholus 13
Born To Raise Hell v
ButtBoy (musician) 22
Butt plug 9, 11, 24, 80, 82, 84

C

Califia, Patrick xv
Catacombs, The xiii, xiv, xviii, xix, xxviii
Chakra xx, xxv, 17, 57
CLAW (Cleveland Leather Awareness Weekend) ii, 9
Colon:
     ascending 5, 14
     descending 5, 6, 13, 14, 16, 27
     sigmoid 5, 6, 11, 16, 19, 27
     transverse 5, 14, 16, 27
Coral Sands Hotel 37
Cox, Harold xv
Cum Hungry 45

D

DC Eagle 53
Delta 13 - 14, 17
Divine Androgyne, The xxi, xxii, 48
Doctor Goodglove 41
Drummer v, xi - xiv, xxix, 70
Dungeon Fist Party 42
Dungeon Fuck Party 42

First Hand

A Boner Book

About The Author:

Tim Brough is living in Philadelphia with his Papa Joel and their house Diva, Sophie, an affectionate Tabby Cat.

He considers himself lucky to have a family that takes some pride in knowing about his writing (even if they aren't necessarily reading them with friends) and also is incredibly proud of the fact that his mother had the courage to stand up to prejudice when confronted.

He'd like to share this family e-mail, from his mother, sent in the summer of 2005.

Our church is going through turmoil because the UCC (United Church of Christ) Synod has approved the marriage of gays. Today, after services, we held an open meeting on this issue. I waited till after about ten people spoke opposing it and threatened to leave the church. I got up and started to speak, saying that at one time interracial marriage was not approved of, blacks had to ride on the back of the bus and then got very emotional. I told them that I am the mother of two openly gay children, and they do not live in a closet but I did (about them). I asked them all to think about children, raising them loving them and then supporting them. Then I sat down. After it was over six women came to me thanking me for speaking. One lady was in tears as her sister is gay and she was struggling with it. I'm sure I stunned many but maybe I opened some hearts.

Tim is the author of two other collections, *Black Gloves, White Magic* and *Sgt Vlengles' Revenge*.

www.TimBrough.com

Photo by Corwin

SUBMIT!

If you would like to see your work in a coming anthology for fisters, email your story or essay to:

FirstHandBook@aol.com.

The follow-up collection to
First Hand: An Erotic Guide To Fisting
is tenatively scheduled for a mid-2006 release.

We're looking for hot fiction and
essays that deal with your thoughts on the art of handballing,

Articles must be submitted in word format via email.

Red Hankies Write,

and we want to put you in print!

All articles become property of
The Nazca Plains Corporation.

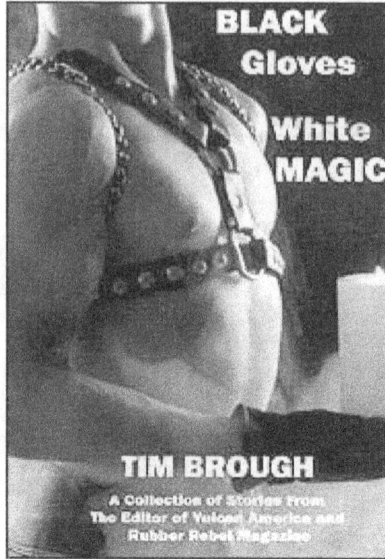

Also available from Tim Brough

Two collections of rough and tumble fiction for men.

**Black Gloves White Magic
and
Sgt Vlengles' Revenge**

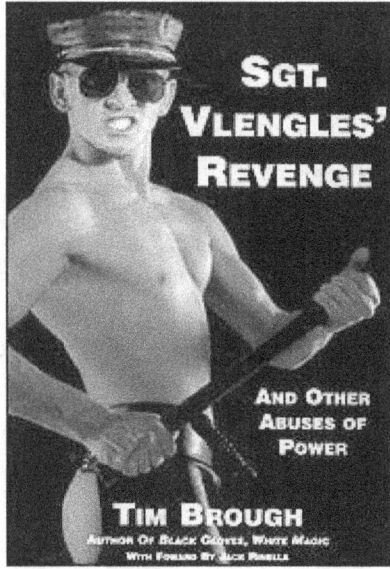

From the pages of Powerplay, Mach, Bunkhouse, Eagle, Cuir, Sandmutopian Guardian, Leather Journal, and the groundbreaking Vulcan America and Rubber Rebel magazines.

www.TimBrough.com

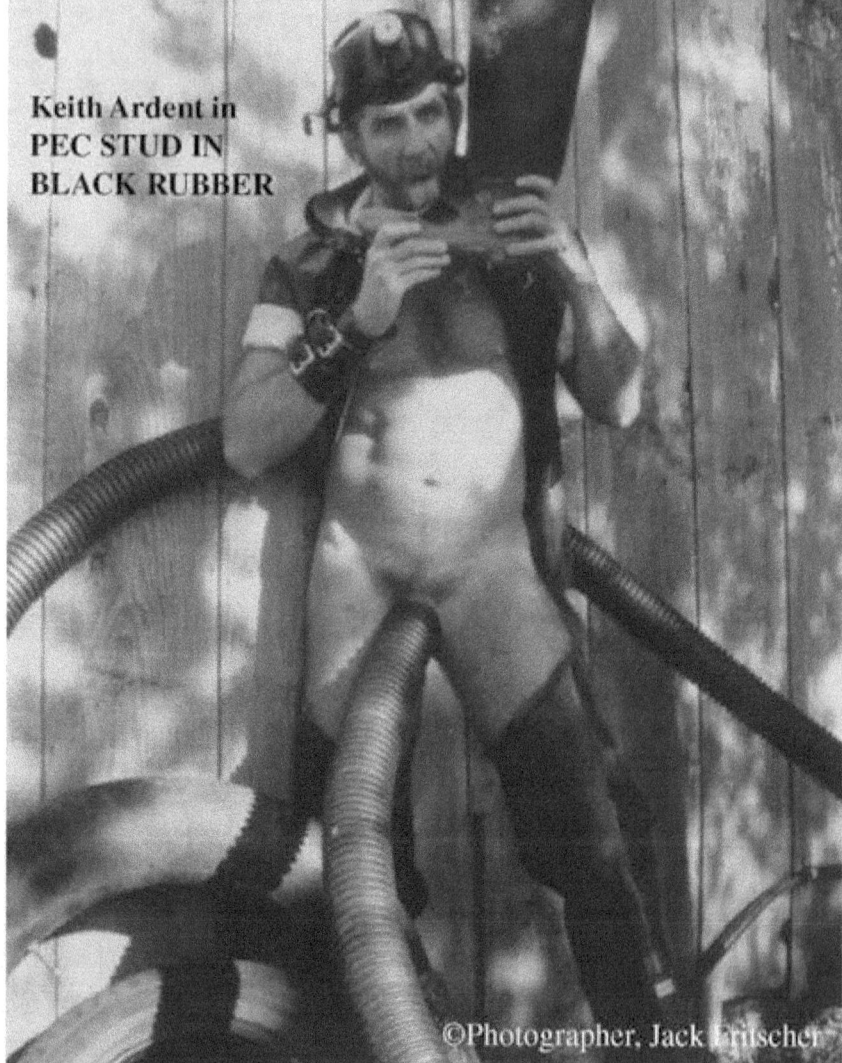

PalmDriveVideo.com
A Fistful of DVD's

Keith Ardent in
PEC STUD IN
BLACK RUBBER

©Photographer, Jack Fritscher

PalmDrivePublishing.com A Fistful of Books

Surf LGBT history, *Drummer* magazine,
Mapplethorpe, & Gay Witchcraft at

JackFritscher.com